SCRAPPY FIREWORK QUILTS

By Edyta Sitar *for* Laundry Basket Quilts

Landauer Publishing, LLC

SCRAPPY FIREWORK QUILTS

By Edyta Sitar *for*
Laundry Basket Quilts

Copyright © 2012 by Landauer Publishing, LLC
Quilt designs copyright © 2011 by Edyta Sitar

This book was designed, produced,
and published by
Landauer Publishing, LLC
3100 NW 101st Street, Urbandale, IA 50322
800-557-2144; www.landauercorp.com

President/Publisher: Jeramy Lanigan Landauer
Vice President of Sales & Administration: Kitty Jacobson
Editor: Jeri Simon
Art Director: Laurel Albright
Technical Editor: Rhonda Matus
Photography: Sue Voegtlin

Library of Congress Control Number: 2011944596
ISBN 13: 978-1-935726-19-7
ISBN 10: 1-935726-19-6
This book is printed on acid-free paper.
Printed in China by
C&C Offset Printing Co., Ltd.
10 9 8 7 6 5 4 3 2 1

Contents

Projects

About the Author...

Edyta Sitar is proud to carry on a family tradition that fabrics and
threads have seamlessly stitched together through the generations.

Her true love for quilting and her quilter's spirit shines through in her classes, workshops,
and presentations. She travels all over sharing her passion with, connecting to and inspiring
quilters of all levels by sharing personal and stimulating stories about the quilts she makes.

Quilting has opened a door to another world for Edyta, one in which she can express herself, create
beautiful designs, and release her artistic passion. The combination of inspiration from nature, a love
for fabric, a keen eye for color, and her family teachings blended into the recipe for developing a
flourishing talent for designing quilts, fabrics, and quilting patterns.

"My children and my husband are my greatest motivation, providing the basis that you can accomplish
anything you want if you just set your mind to it. Being able to do what I love and share this love with
others is the greatest feeling and reward I could imagine! This is the Cinderella dream for me."

As the owner and co-founder of Laundry Basket Quilts, her work has been published in
magazines world-wide and her quilts have received numerous awards.

Edyta resides in Marshall, Michigan with her husband and children where she enjoys creating
beautiful patterns for Laundry Basket Quilts and designing splendid fabrics for MODA.

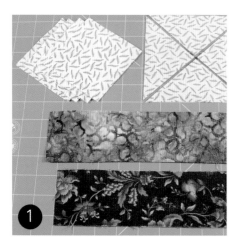

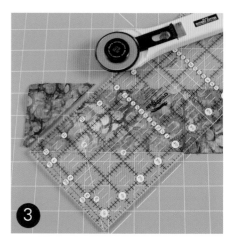

To make an 8-pointed star, you will need four fabric background squares, four quarter-square setting triangles and two fabric strips.

To practice making an 8-pointed star, cut (2) 2-3/4" strips, (4) 3-3/4" background squares and (1) 5-1/4" square cut twice on the diagonal for quarter-square setting triangles.

Lay the two fabric strips right sides together.

Place a ruler on the fabric strips, aligning the ruler's 45-degree line with the bottom edge of the strips. Trim along the ruler's edge to create a 45-degree angle.

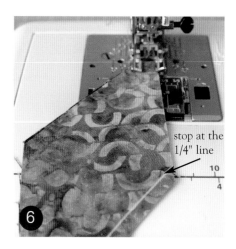

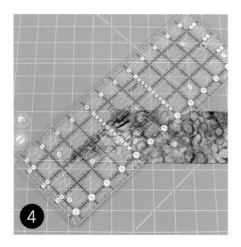

The width of the fabric strips will determine where the ruler should be placed to cut the diamond shape. For example, the fabric strips above are 2-3/4" wide so we will measure and cut 2-3/4" from the angled edge.

Cut four sets of diamonds from the layered strips. Do not separate. Working with the same fabric on top, mark each top diamond with a 1/4" line.

Note: *The lines need to be in the same position on each diamond.*

stop at the 1/4" line

10

4

Begin sewing at the tip of the diamond. Sew to the 1/4" line, stop and backstitch. Sew the remaining sets of diamonds in the same manner.

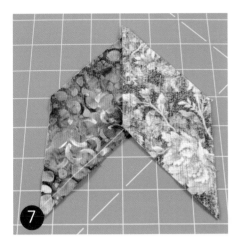

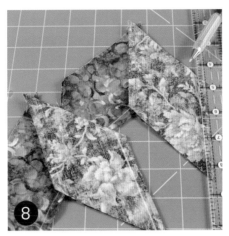

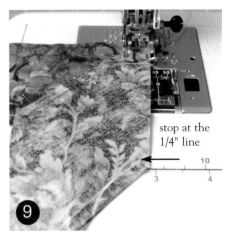

Press the seam allowances to the left on the four sets of diamonds.

Lay two sets of diamonds right sides together. Mark the top diamonds with a 1/4" line as shown.

Begin sewing at the tip of the diamond. Sew to the 1/4" line, stop and backstitch. Sew the remaining set of diamonds in the same manner. You should now have two star halves.

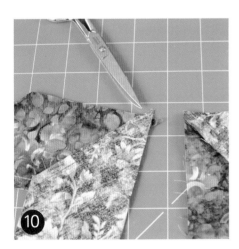

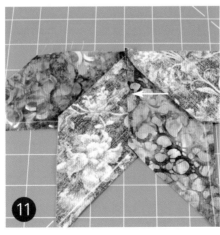

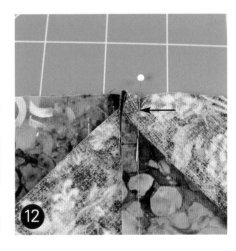

Before pressing the seam allowance, trim the "bunny ears".

Press the seam allowances to the left on both star halves.

Lay the two star halves right sides together. Pin at the point where the threads cross in the center forming an "X".

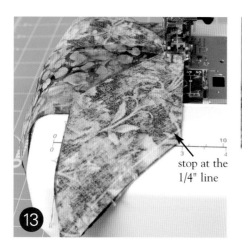

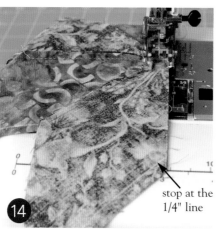
stop at the
1/4" line

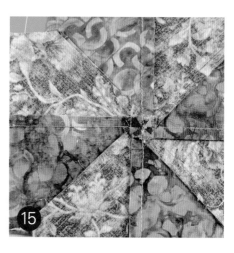
stop at the
1/4" line

Begin sewing at the "X" down to the 1/4" line, stop and backstitch.

Flip the star over and begin sewing from the "X" to the 1/4" line. Stop and backstitch.

Open the center seam and press seam allowances to the left.

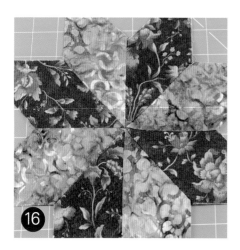

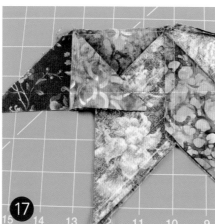

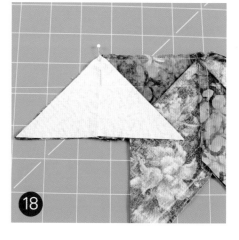

The star is now ready for the background pieces to be set in.

Fold the star in half, right sides together. Pull a star point back as shown.

Note: *Always begin with the setting triangles. You may find it helpful to lightly crease the center of the triangles. This will help align the setting triangle with the center of the star points.*

Lay a setting triangle on the star point, right sides together. The center of the setting triangle will be even with the center. Pin at the top, or pivot, point. The pivot point should be 1/4" away from the tip of the triangle.

Note: *You may wish to mark a 1/4" line along the edge of the setting triangles. The line will act as a guide, along with the pin, to mark the pivot point.*

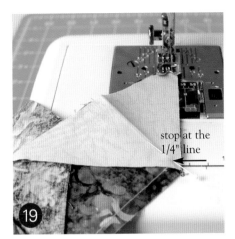

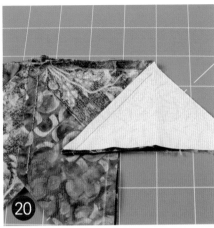

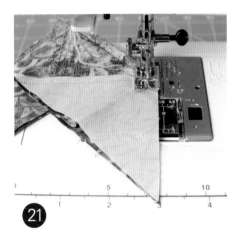

Sew from the diamond tip to the pivot point. Stop and backstitch.

Reposition the star point so the unstitched edge is aligned with the setting triangle.

Begin sewing at the pivot point, backstitching to secure the first stitches. Continue sewing to the tip of the triangle.

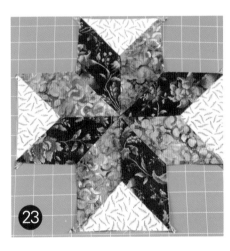

Open the star block and finger press the seam allowances toward the star to complete the "Y" seam.

Set in the remaining three triangles.

9

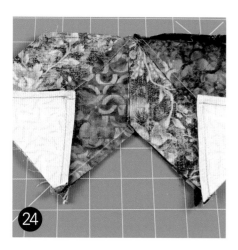

To set in the background squares, fold the star block in half, right sides together.

Pull back a corner of the block as shown.

Lay a background square on the block corner, right sides together. Place a pin at the pivot point. The pivot point should be 1/4" away from the tip of the square.

Note: *You may wish to mark a 1/4" line along the edge of the background squares. The line will act as a guide, along with the pin, to mark the pivot point.*

stop at the 1/4" line

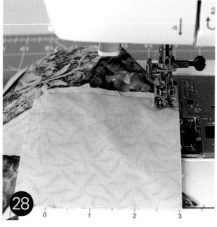

Sew from the outside edge of the square to the pivot point. Stop, backstitch and remove the pin.

Reposition the block corner so the unstitched edge is aligned with the background square. Begin sewing at the pivot point, backstitching to secure the stitches. Stitch to the edge of the square.

Finger press the seam allowances toward the star. Continue to set in the remaining background squares. Press the seam allowances toward the star.

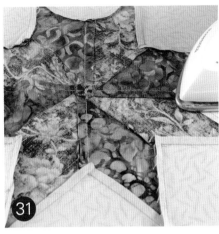

Trim the "bunny ears".

Press the block from the back. Press all seams toward the star.

Square up the finished block, if needed.

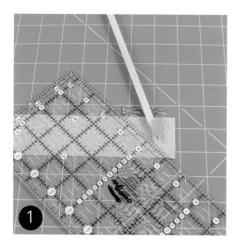

Cut 1-3/4" strips. The number of strips to cut will be determined by the project instructions.

Lay one of the strips, right side up, on a flat surface. Place a second strip, wrong side up, on the first strip as shown. Draw a diagonal line from corner to corner on the top strip.

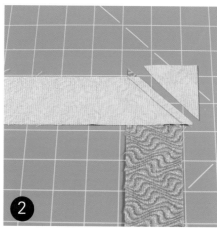

Sew on the drawn line. Trim the fabric 1/4" away from the sewn line.

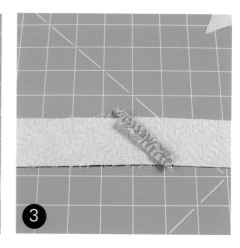

Press the seam allowances open. Continue until all the strips have been joined into one long continuous binding strip. Trim the "bunny ears".

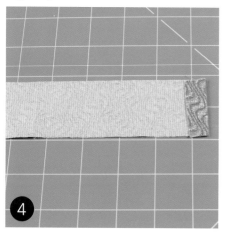

Fold one end of the binding strip over 1/2" and press.

Note: *There are alternate methods to binding a quilt. This is how my grandmother taught me to do it. I love the clean look and ease of binding this way. This is a perfect method for lighter weight binding and especially smaller projects.*

Align the raw edge of the binding strip with the raw edge of the quilted quilt top, batting and backing, right sides together. Begin sewing at the folded end of the binding strip. I generally begin my binding near the center point of the quilt top side edge.

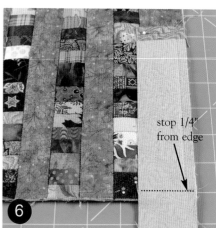

stop 1/4" from edge

Use a 1/4" seam allowance and sew the binding strip to the quilted quilt top, batting and backing. Stop 1/4" from the next edge of the quilted quilt top, batting and backing and backstitch.

Here's a Tip

I like to fold and lightly crease my binding at the 1/4" stopping point. You may also mark the stopping point with a pin.

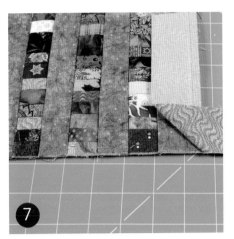

7

Fold the binding strip to create a 45-degree angle.

8

start sewing at edge

Fold the binding strip back over and align with the raw edge of the quilted quilt top, batting and backing. Start sewing at the edge with a 1/4" seam allowance. Continue sewing the binding strip to the quilt top, mitering each corner.

9

When you have reached the beginning point of the binding strip, cut the ending strip leaving 1/2" overlap. Sew a few stitches over the starting stitches.

10

Fold the binding strip to the stitched seam line. Iron or finger press the folded strip around the entire quilt top to create a crease.

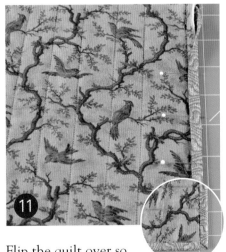

11

Flip the quilt over so the backing is facing up. Turn the binding to the quilt back. Using a slipstitch sew it in place and fold the corners as you come to them. If you wish, use pins or binding clips to hold the binding in place as you stitch.

12

The result will be a flat, less bulky binding that still provides a double layer of protection for the edge of your beautiful quilt projects.

This style of appliqué has become my personal favorite. With a little patience and the right materials you can achieve excellent results in a short period of time. I also find it to be a relaxing and enjoyable technique.

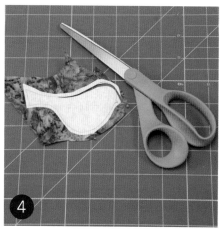

Supplies—Light fusible webbing, pressing sheet, sharp scissors, traced block layout, reversed appliqué pieces, pencil, cotton thread for sewing the **buttonhole stitch** and for the bobbin (I prefer Aurifil™ 2370 in the bobbin), nylon invisible thread for sewing the **zigzag stitch**, embroidery 75/11 needle for machine, background fabric, and desired appliqué fabric

To prepare the appliqués, place the fusible webbing, paper side up on the reversed appliqué shapes. Trace each appliqué shape, including any dashed lines, onto the fusible webbing. Mark each shape with its corresponding letter to help you place the pieces correctly on the layout.

Note: *All shapes in the book are conveniently reversed for this technique.*

Cut out the appliqué shapes from the fusible webbing leaving at least 1/8" of fusible webbing around the outside of each shape. You may cut the fusible webbing from the center of the larger pieces, if you wish.

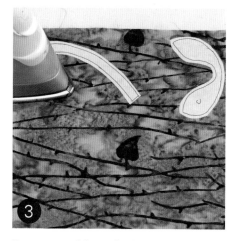

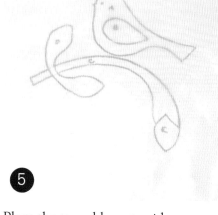

Press your fabrics before fusing to be sure there are no wrinkles or creases. Fuse each appliqué shape by pressing it to the wrong side of the desired color fabric following manufacturer's directions on fusible webbing.

Note: *Do not overheat fusible webbing.*

Cut the appliqué shapes out **exactly** on the traced line. Achieve nice smooth edges by using the back blades of a sharp scissors and making long cuts.

Place the traced layout guide under the pressing sheet on an ironing board. Proceed to prepare the appliqué pieces to place on the background.

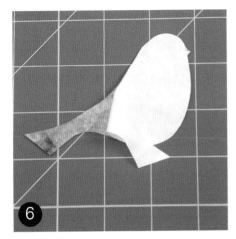

6

7

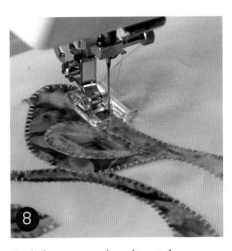

8

Peel the fusible webbing paper from each shape.

Note: If you crease the edge of the paper it will peel off easier.

After all the paper is peeled off, place each fabric appliquéd shape on top of the pressing sheet, following the layout underneath as a placement guide. Press the appliqué shapes together only where the fabric appliqués overlap. Press gently to secure these pieces together. Make sure all your pieces stay on the layout and use it as your guide.

Note: Remember the dashed lines indicate where the fabric shapes overlap each other.

Peel the group of appliqué shapes from the pressing sheet and place where desired on your block. Press in place. Stitch around all edges of the appliqués with a buttonhole or zigzag stitch.

Here's a Tip
To lock your stitches when sewing, overlap the beginning and ending stitches. Gently pull all the thread to the back once the block is completed.

Stitch Style

Buttonhole stitch around the edge of the appliqué.

Note: Actual size of stitch is shown.

Top thread - cotton 50 wt.
Bobbin thread - cotton to match background
Needle - Embroidery 75/11
Stitch - Buttonhole
Tension - Slightly lower so no bobbin thread shows on top of appliqué

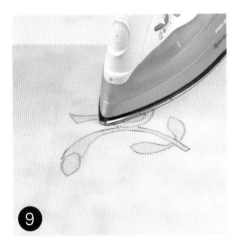

9

10

When you have completed stitching the shapes to the fabric, gently press from the back. This will heal any holes left by the needle. Be careful that the iron is not too hot. You don't want to overpress and melt the fusible web through the fabric.

The appliquéd block is now ready to add to your project.

Note: Fusible appliqué is always easier when done in sections and then sewn to the quilt top. You can add more appliqué pieces if desired.

Stitch Style

Zigzag stitch around the edge of the appliqué.

Note: Actual size of stitch is shown.

Top thread - nylon invisible
Bobbin thread - cotton to match background
Needle - Embroidery 75/11
Stitch - Zigzag
Tension - Varies from 0-1 on top depending on sewing machine

When a project calls for many half-square triangles or I am exchanging triangles with friends the Triangle Exchange Paper makes the process of creating them quick, accurate and easy.

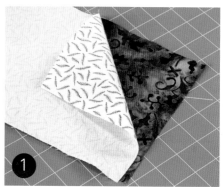

Supplies—Laundry Basket Quilts Half Square Triangle Exchange Paper, cotton thread (I prefer Aurifil™ 2370 for color; it blends beautifully with any fabric), acrylic ruler, rotary cutter, cutting mat, pins, and desired light and dark fabric

Cut a 6-1/2" x 21" rectangle from each of the light and dark fabric pieces. Place the light fabric rectangle on the dark fabric rectangle, right sides together.

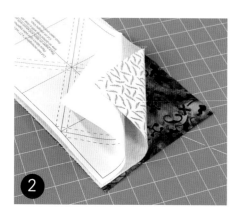

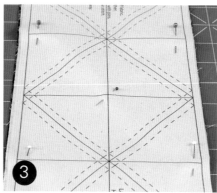

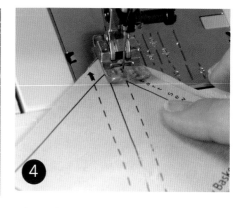

Lay the Triangle Exchange Paper, with printed lines facing up, on top of the light fabric piece.

Note: *The half-square triangle's seam allowance will automatically go toward the dark fabric when the exchange paper is placed on the light fabric.*

Pin the paper in place using a hopscotch pattern—two pins in the outside triangle markings and one pin in the center. Do not pin over the dashed lines. You will be sewing on these lines.

Note: *Use a sharp 80/12 needle and cotton thread in your sewing machine and sew with a close stitch. I usually set my machine stitch to 1.5. A closer stitch allows the paper to tear away more easily.*

Place the corner of the paper marked "Start Sewing" under your presser foot and begin sewing on the dashed line. Sew until you reach the end of the first continuous dashed line.

Note: *Use the needle down function on your machine while sewing through the paper and fabric. It will allow you to turn the corners without shifting the paper and fabric.*

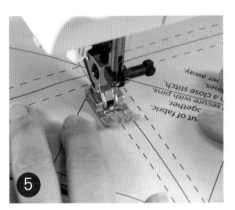

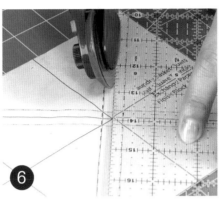

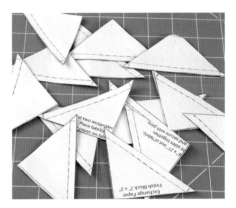

Turn the paper and fabric and follow the arrow to sew the remaining dashed line. Remove the pins.

Using a rotary cutter and acrylic ruler, cut on the solid lines of the Triangle Exchange Paper. Each sheet of Triangle Exchange Paper will make 28 half-square triangles.

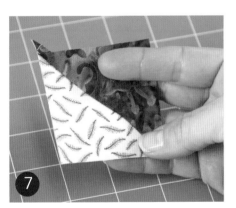

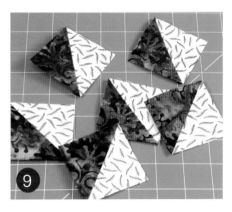

With the paper still attached, press the half-square triangle blocks open. The seam allowance should go toward the darker fabric. Trim the "bunny ears" from the block.

Perforate the Triangle Exchange Paper by pinching the center of the light fabric triangle and the paper. Remove the paper by tearing from the center to the outside edges of the block.

Your triangles are now ready to be used in any of your favorite projects.

Strip panels are easy to make and a great way to use all those leftover strips and fabric scraps. Share strips with friends achieve a beautiful one-of-a-kind color scheme.

Supplies—Fabric or fabric scraps, cotton thread (I prefer Aurifil™ 2370 for color; it blends beautifully with any fabric), acrylic ruler, rotary cutter, and cutting mat. Even when choosing fabric scraps remember to follow my Rule of Five. Pick a big print, medium print, small print, stripe, and polka dot. This will give your project a beautiful look and a nice texture.

Straighten fabric edges before cutting your strips. Cut fabric strips between 1" and 2-1/2" wide. Vary the width of the strips if desired. Always cut from selvage to selvage. Due to the differences in fabric width, the length of your strips will be between 40" and 44".

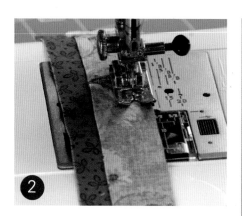

Layer two strips, right sides together and sew along one long edge, using a 1/4" seam allowance. Press the seams in one direction.

Here's a Tip
Take advantage of wonderful precut fabrics such as Jelly Rolls™ and Honey Buns™ from Moda. You will get a variety of colors in ready to sew precut strips. Fat quarter bundles also work well for scrappy projects.

Place a third strip on the strip panel aligning the long edges. Begin sewing the third strip at the opposite end where you joined the first two strips. Press seams in same direction as first two strips. **You may wish to flip the fabric so the strip panel is laying on top when sewing. This will keep the strip panel from 'waving'.**

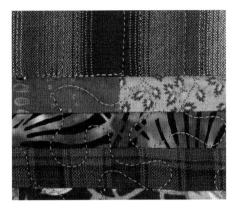

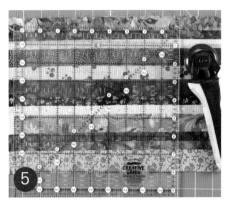

Here's a Tip

If you have strips that are uneven or too short for the strip panel but are the same width, sew them together until they equal 40"-44" in length. Use a matching or contrasting fabric strip to add a scrappy look to your finished project.

Continue adding strips to the strip panel, aligning long edges and alternating the direction they are sewn together. Press all seams in the same direction.

The final strip panel should be no larger than 18" x approximately 40"-44" (fabric length will vary). A strip panel this size is easy to sew and will accommodate any of the shapes and templates you need to cut. If you have chosen a project, the strip panel should be approximately 1" larger than your block or template size. With your ruler, cut out the size of blocks needed for your project.

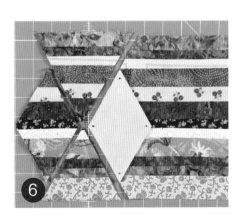

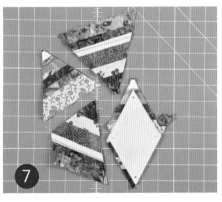

If using a template, lay the chosen template over the strip panel. Be sure the tip of the template is not laying on a seam line. Cut around the template to create the shape needed for your project.

Use every bit of the strip panel by taking the triangles left over from cutting the diamonds and piecing them, right sides together. Press open and place the diamond template on top. Cut around the template to create another diamond.

Full-size templates for each project may be found in the book. Acrylic templates, as well as Appliqué Silhouettes sheets, may be purchased at **www.laundrybasketquilts.com.**

QUILTER'S SCHOOLHOUSE QUILT

Materials

- 3-1/4 yards total assorted light prints and batiks for blocks, setting and corner triangles, and first border
- 1/3 yard total assorted dark prints and batiks for tree and schoolhouse blocks
- 1/3 yard total assorted dark brown prints and batiks for flower and schoolhouse blocks
- 1/4 yard total assorted medium-to-dark pink prints and batiks for flower blocks
- 1/2 yard total assorted dark green prints and batiks for flower blocks
- 2 – 9" x 22" (fat eighths) or 1/8 yard pieces of assorted brown batiks for tree blocks
- Variety of dark blue 1" and 1-1/4" x 21" print and batik strips (approximately 8 strips) for schoolhouse block
- 2 assorted 1" x 11" dark blue print or batik strips for schoolhouse block
- 1 – 2-1/2" x 5-1/4" rectangle of dark red print for schoolhouse block
- 10 – 1-1/4" squares of assorted yellow prints and batiks for schoolhouse block
- 1/4 yard blue print for second border
- 1/3 yard brown batik for third border
- 1 yard dark brown print for fourth border
- 1/2 yard dark batik for binding

- 3" x 14" rectangle of brown print for stem appliqués
- Assorted green print and batik scraps for leaf appliqués
- 3" x 5" rectangle of blue print for bird appliqué
- 3-1/3 yards backing fabric
- 60" x 80" batting

Finished flower block: 9" square
Finished tree block: 11-1/4" x 19-3/4"
Finished schoolhouse block: 15-1/2" x 19-3/4"
Finished quilt: 53-1/2" x 73-1/4"

Quantities are for 40/44"-wide, 100% cotton fabrics. Measurements include 1/4" seam allowances. Sew with right sides together unless otherwise stated.

NOTES: Follow the instructions given to make half-square triangles or refer to pages 16 - 17 for instructions on using Laundry Basket Quilts Half Square Triangle Exchange Paper.

Refer to Strip Panels on pages 18 - 19 to sew together the dark blue 1" and 1-1/4" x 21" print and batik strips to form a strip panel approximately 5" x 21". Press seams in one direction.

CUT THE FABRICS

Note: Cut one 6-3/4" square and the 2" x 16" strip from the same light print or batik fabric.

From assorted light prints and batiks, cut:

2 – 14" squares, cutting each diagonally in an X for a total of 8 setting triangles

1 – 16" x 8-1/4" rectangle

2 – 7-1/4" squares, cutting each in half diagonally for a total of 4 corner triangles

4 – 6-3/4" squares, cutting each in half diagonally for a total of 8 I triangles

13 – 5-3/8" squares, cutting each in half diagonally for a total of 26 C triangles

13 – 5" squares, cutting each in half diagonally for a total of 26 D triangles

1 – 4-7/8" square, cut in half diagonally for a total of 2 H triangles

1 – 4-1/8" square, cut in half diagonally for a total of 2 K triangles

2 shapes using template on page 28

2 reversed shapes using template on page 28

14 – 2-7/8" squares

6 – 2-1/2" squares

2 – 3" x 7-1/2" rectangles

69 – 2-3/8" squares

26 – 2-3/8" squares, cutting each in half diagonally for a total of 52 A triangles

1 – 2" x 16" strip
1 – 2" x 6" rectangle
1 – 2" x 4" rectangle
5 – 1-3/4" x 42" first border strips
18 – 1-1/2" squares
8 – 1-1/4" squares
4 – 1-1/8" x 2" rectangles
8 – 1-1/8" x 1" rectangles
From assorted dark prints and batiks, cut:
14 – 2-7/8" squares
6 – 2-7/8" squares, cutting each in half diagonally for a total of 12 E triangles
18 – 1-1/2" squares
4 – 1-1/4" squares
4 – 1-1/8" x 4" strips
8 – 1-1/8" x 1" rectangles
From assorted dark brown prints and batiks, cut:
49 – 2-3/8" squares
4 – 2-3/8" squares, cutting each in half diagonally for a total of 8 J triangles
From assorted medium-to-dark pink prints and batiks, cut:
20 – 2-3/8" squares
From assorted dark green prints and batiks, cut:
20 – 3-7/8" squares, cutting each in half diagonally for a total of 40 B triangles
13 – 1" x 8" strips
From each assorted brown batik fat eighth, cut:
1 – 4-7/8" square, cut in half diagonally for a total of 2 G triangles
1 – 3-3/8" x 6-1/8" rectangle
1 – 3-1/4" square, cut diagonally in an X for a total of 4 F triangles
From the strip panel, cut:
2 – 4-3/4" x 3" rectangles
2 – 1-3/4" x 2-3/4" rectangles
2 – 1-1/4" x 2-3/4" rectangles

From blue print, cut:
5 – 1" x 42" second border strips
From brown batik, cut:
6 – 1-1/2" x 42" third border strips
From dark brown print, cut:
6 – 5-1/4" x 42" fourth border strips
From dark batik, cut:
7 – 1-3/4" x 42" binding strips
From backing, cut:
2 – 40-1/2" x 60" rectangles

Making Half-Square Triangles

1. With right sides together, layer a light print or batik 2-3/8" square with a dark brown print or batik 2-3/8" square. Draw a diagonal line across the wrong side of the light print or batik square.

2. Sew 1/4" on both sides of the drawn line. Cut apart on the drawn line. Press seam toward the dark triangle. The half-square triangles should measure 2" square. Repeat Steps 1 - 2 to make a total of 98 brown/light half-square triangles; 91 for flower blocks and 7 for schoolhouse block.

MAKE 98
HALF-SQUARE TRIANGLES

3. Repeat Steps 1 - 2 with the medium-to-dark pink print or batik 2-3/8" squares and the remaining light print or batik 2-3/8" squares to make a total of 40 pink/light half-square triangles for flower blocks. The half-square triangles should measure 2" square. There will be one unused pink/light half-square triangle.

MAKE 40
HALF-SQUARE TRIANGLES

4. Repeat Steps 1 - 2 with dark print or batik 2-7/8" squares and the light print or batik 2-7/8" squares to make a total of 28 dark/light half-square triangles for tree blocks. The half-square triangles should measure 2-1/2" square. There will be one unused dark/light half-square triangle.

MAKE 28
HALF-SQUARE TRIANGLES

Assemble Flower Blocks

1. Lay out three assorted pink/light half-square triangles, three assorted brown/light half-square triangles, two light print or batik A triangles, and one dark green print or batik B triangle as shown. Sew half-square triangles and A triangles together in rows. Press seams in one direction, alternating the direction from row to row. Sew the rows

together; press. Add the dark green print or batik B triangle to complete the flower section; press seam toward B.

2. Lay out two assorted brown/light half-square triangles, one light print or batik A triangle, one dark green print or batik B triangle, and one light print or batik C triangle as shown. Sew the half-square triangles and A triangle together in a row. Press seams in one direction. Sew the row to the dark green print or batik B triangle. Press seam toward B. Add the light print or batik C triangle to complete the right leaf section; press seam toward C.

3. Lay out two assorted brown/light half-square triangles, one light print or batik A triangle, one dark green print or batik B triangle, and one light print or batik C triangle as shown. Sew the half-square triangles and A triangle together in a row. Press seams in one direction. Sew the row to the dark green print or batik B triangle. Press seam

toward B. Add the light print or batik C triangle to complete the left leaf section; press seam toward C.

4. Fold two light print or batik D triangles and one dark green print or batik 1" x 8" strip in half to find the centers. Align the centers and sew to complete the stem section. Press seams toward strip. Trim the strip ends so stem section measures 5" x 5".

5. Sew the flower and right leaf sections together for the top half; press seam toward right leaf section. Sew the left leaf and stem sections together for the bottom half; press seam toward left leaf section. Sew the top and bottom halves together to complete one flower block. Press seam toward bottom half.

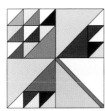

MAKE 13

6. Repeat Steps 1 - 5 to make a total of 13 flower blocks. There will be one unused dark green print or batik B triangle.

ASSEMBLE TREE BLOCKS

1. Sew together the light print or batik and the dark print or batik 1-1/2" squares together in pairs. Press seam toward dark square. Make 18 pairs.

MAKE 18

2. Sew two pairs together, reversing the light and dark fabrics to make one four-patch unit. Press seam in one direction. Repeat to make nine four-patch units.

MAKE 9

3. Lay out four assorted dark/light half-square triangles, two four-patch units, and three light print or batik 2-1/2" squares as shown. Sew the pieces together in rows. Press the seams in one direction, alternating direction from row to row. Sew the rows together to complete the top leaf section; press. Make a second top leaf section, using five dark/light half-square triangles, one four-patch unit, and three light 2-1/2" squares.

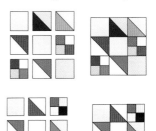

4. Lay out five assorted dark/light half-square triangles, one four-patch unit, and three dark print or batik E triangles as shown. Sew the pieces together in rows. Press the seams in one direction, alternating direction from row to row. Sew the rows together to complete one right leaf section; press. Repeat to make a second right leaf section.

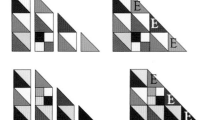

5. Lay out five assorted dark/light half-square triangles, one four-patch unit, and three dark print or batik E triangles as shown. Sew the pieces together in rows. Press the seams in one direction, alternating direction from row to row. Sew the rows together to complete one left leaf section; press. Make a second left leaf section, using three dark/light half-square triangles, three four-patch units, and three dark print or batik E triangles.

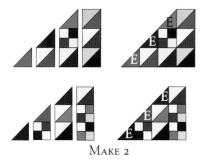

MAKE 2

6. Lay out one brown batik 3-3/8" x 6-1/8" rectangle,

2 brown batik F triangles, one brown batik G triangle, one light print or batik H triangle, one template shape, and one template shape reversed as shown. There will be two unused F triangles and one unused G triangle.

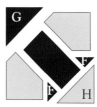

Note: A single dark batik was used for all trunk pieces in each block.

7. Sew a brown batik F triangle to the template shaped pieces as shown. Press seams away from the triangles. Sew these to the long edges of the dark batik 3-3/8" x 6-1/8" rectangle. Press seams toward rectangle.

8. Add a brown batik G triangle to the top of the piece sewn in Step 7 and a light H triangle to the bottom of the piece to complete one trunk section. Press seams toward triangles.

9. Repeat Steps 6 - 8 to make a second trunk section.

10. Sew the top leaf and right leaf sections together for the top half; press seam toward top leaf section. Sew the left leaf and trunk sections together for the bottom half; press seam toward trunk section. Sew the top and bottom halves together to complete the tree section. Press seam toward bottom half. Repeat with the remaining leaf and trunk sections to make a second tree section.

11. Sew four light print or batik I triangles to the corners of the tree section to complete one tree block. Press seams toward the triangles. The block should measure 11-3/4" x 20-1/4". Repeat for second block.

Note: To make the quilt as shown, match the color of the I triangle at the bottom inside corner of each tree block to the color of the 2" x 16" strip at the bottom of the schoolhouse block.

ASSEMBLE SCHOOLHOUSE BLOCK

1. Sew together five assorted yellow print or batik 1-1/4" squares and four assorted light print or batik 1-1/4" squares in three rows of three as shown. Press seams toward yellow squares. Sew the rows together to complete one window. Repeat to make second window.

MAKE 2

2. Sew strip panel 1-1/4" x 2-3/4" rectangles and 1-3/4" x 2-3/4" rectangles to opposite sides of the windows from Step 1 as shown. Press seams toward windows.

3. Add strip panel 4-3/4" x 3" rectangles to bottom edge of window sections. Press seams toward rectangles.

4. Sew together the window sections and the dark red print 2-1/2" x 5-1/4" rectangle. Press seams toward rectangle. Sew two dark blue print or batik 1" x 11" strips to the top of the house. Press seams toward strips.

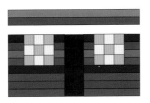

5. Lay out seven brown/light half-square triangles and seven dark brown J triangles in rows as shown. Sew the pieces together in rows. Press seams in one direction, alternating the direction from row to row. Sew the rows together to complete the roof; press. There will be one unused J triangle.

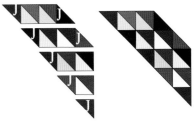

6. Sew light print or batik K triangles to the roof section. Press seams toward triangles. Sew the roof section to house. Press seam toward house.

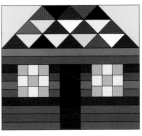

7. Sew together four assorted dark print or batik 1-1/4" squares in pairs. Press seams in alternating directions. Sew the pairs together to make one four-patch unit for the chimney. Press seam in one direction.

8. Sew together the chimney from Step 7 and the light print or batik 2" x 6" and 2" x 4" rectangles for the chimney section. Press seams away from chimney. Add the chimney section to roof. Press seam toward chimney section.

9. Lay out two dark print or batik 1-1/8" x 4" strips, four dark print or batik 1-1/8" x 1" rectangles, two light print or batik 1-1/8" x 2" rectangles, and four light print or batik 1-1/8" x 1" rectangles. Sew the pieces together in vertical rows. Press seams toward dark rectangles. Sew the rows together to complete one fence section. Press seams toward dark strips. Repeat to make second fence section.

MAKE 2

10. Sew the light print or batik 3" x 7-1/2" rectangles to the top edges of the fence sections to make the left and right side sections. Press seams

toward rectangles. Add side sections to opposite edges of house. Press seam toward side sections.

11. Sew light print or batik 16" x 8-1/4" rectangle to top edge of house and light print or batik 2" x 16" strip to bottom edge. Press seams away from house. The schoolhouse block should measure 16" x 20-1/4".

APPLIQUÉ THE SCHOOLHOUSE BLOCK

1. Trace the appliqué patterns on page 29. Prepare the appliqué pieces using the instructions on pages 14 - 15 or the appliqué method of your choice.
   From brown print, cut:
   1 of pattern A (stem)
   From assorted green prints and batiks, cut:
   9 of pattern B (leaf)
   From blue print, cut:
   1 of pattern C (bird)
2. Cut the stem into two pieces. Gently curve stem pieces on the schoolhouse block and trim to desired length, referring to the Appliqué Placement Diagram as a guide. Place the leaf and bird appliqué pieces along the stems. Appliqué the shapes in place using your favorite method. A narrow zigzag stitch was used along the edges of each of the appliqué pieces.

Quilter's Schoolhouse Quilt

ASSEMBLE THE QUILT CENTER

1. Sew together the schoolhouse block and the two tree blocks to make the top section of quilt center.
2. Lay out 13 flower blocks and eight light print or batik setting triangles in diagonal rows.
3. Sew together pieces in each diagonal row. Press seams in one direction, alternating direction from row to row.
4. Join rows. Press seams in one direction. Add light print or batik corner triangles to complete the bottom section of the quilt center. Press seams toward the corner triangles.
5. Referring to the Quilt Top Assembly Diagram, join the top and bottom sections to complete the quilt center. Press seam in one direction.

ADD THE BORDERS

1. Piece the light print 1-3/4" x 42" first border strips to make the following: 2 – 1-3/4" x 58-1/4" for sides and 2 – 1-3/4" x 41" for top and bottom.
2. Referring to the Quilt Top Assembly Diagram, sew the side first border strips to the quilt center. Press seams toward the border. Add the top and bottom first border strips to the quilt center. Press seams toward the border.
3. Piece the blue print 1" x 42" second border strips to make the following: 2 – 1" x 60-3/4" for sides and 2 – 1" x 42" for top and bottom.
4. Add the side second border strips to the quilt top. Press seams toward the second border. Add the top and bottom second border strips to the quilt top. Press seams toward the second border.
5. Piece the brown batik 1-1/2" x 42" third border strips to make the following: 2 – 1-1/2" x 61-3/4" for sides and 2 – 1-1/2" x 44" for top and bottom.
6. Add the side third border strips to the quilt top. Press seams toward the third border. Add the top and bottom third border strips to the quilt top. Press seams toward the third border.
7. Piece the dark brown print 5-1/4" x 42" fourth border strips to make the following: 2 – 5-1/4" x 73-1/4" for sides and 2 – 5-1/4" x 44" for top and bottom.
8. Add the top and bottom fourth border strips to the quilt top. Press seams toward the fourth border. Add the side fourth border strips to the quilt top. Press seams toward the fourth border.

QUILT CENTER TOP SECTION

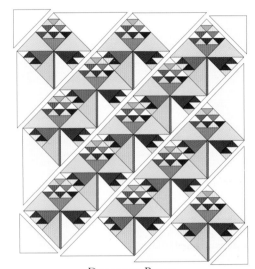

DIAGONAL ROWS

QUILT TOP ASSEMBLY DIAGRAM

Quilter's Schoolhouse Quilt

COMPLETE THE QUILT

1. Sew together the 40-1/2" x 60" backing rectangles along one long edge, using a 1/2" seam allowance. Press the seam allowance open.
2. Layer quilt top, batting, and pieced backing.

3. Quilt as desired. The quilt was stitched using neutral thread for an allover swirl pattern.
4. Bind with dark batik binding strips, referring to the binding instructions on pages 12 - 13.

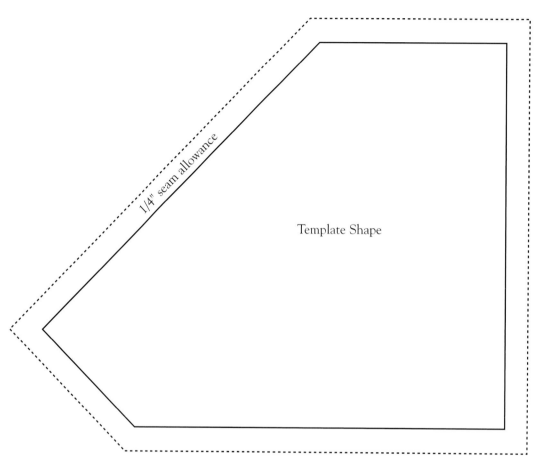

1/4" seam allowance

Template Shape

Quilter's Schoolhouse Templates

These shapes have been reversed for fusible appliqué.

Stem
(A)
Cut 1

Bird
(C)
Cut 1

Leaf
(B)
Cut 9

Quilter's Schoolhouse Appliqué Placement Diagram

(C)

(B)

(B)

(B)

(B)

(B)

(B)

(B)

(B)

(B)

Quilter's Schoolhouse Quilt
Designed and pieced by Edyta Sitar for Laundry Basket Quilts

A handful of scraps becomes a window of opportunity for quilters.

BASKET OF POSIES WALLHANGING

Materials

- 23" x 19" rectangle of light batik for appliqué foundation
- 1/4 yard dark batik for binding
- 10" square of dark plaid for basket appliqué
- 3 – 4" x 10" rectangles of assorted brown batiks for stem appliqués
- Assorted green print and batik scraps for leaf appliqués
- Assorted blue print and batik scraps for flower appliqués
- Pink batik and rust print scraps for flower appliqués
- Dark pink batik scrap for bud appliqué
- Assorted gold print and batik scraps for flower center appliqués
- 27" x 23" backing fabric
- 27" x 23" batting

Finished wallhanging: 21" x 17"

Quantities are for 40/44"-wide, 100% cotton fabrics.

CUT THE FABRICS

From dark batik, cut:
2 – 1-3/4" x 42" binding strips

CUT AND ASSEMBLE THE APPLIQUÉ WALLHANGING

1. Trace the appliqué patterns on pages 34 - 35. Prepare the appliqué pieces using the instructions on pages 14 - 15 or the appliqué method of your choice.

From dark plaid, cut:
1 of pattern A on the bias (basket)

From assorted brown batiks, cut:
1 of pattern B (branch)
1 of pattern C (stem)
1 of pattern D (stem)
1 of pattern E (stem)
5 of pattern F (stem)
1 of pattern G (stem)

From assorted green print and batik scraps, cut:
8 of pattern H (medium leaf)
2 of pattern I (large leaf)
2 of pattern I reversed (large leaf)
3 of pattern J (double leaf)
2 of pattern K (double leaf)

From assorted blue print and batik scraps, cut:
10 of pattern L (medium flower)
6 of pattern M (small flower)

From pink batik and rust print scraps, cut:
2 of pattern N (large flower)

From dark pink batik, cut:
1 of pattern O (bud)

From gold prints and batiks, cut:
4 of pattern P (flower center)

2. Position the appliqué pieces on the 23" x 19" light batik foundation rectangle. Trim some of the F pieces to vary the length of the stems. Appliqué the shapes in place using your favorite method. A narrow zigzag stitch was used along the edges of each of the appliqué shapes. Press the appliquéd rectangle from the back. Center and trim it to 21" x 17".

COMPLETE THE WALLHANGING

1. Layer wallhanging top, batting, and backing.
2. Quilt as desired. The wallhanging was quilted using neutral thread, stitched closely around the appliqué shapes. The background was filled with a crackling pattern.
3. Bind with dark batik binding strips, referring to the Binding instructions on pages 12 - 13.

Basket of Posies Wallhanging Templates

These shapes have been reversed for fusible appliqué.

Small Flower
(M)
Cut 6

Medium Flower
(L)
Cut 10

Longest Curved
Stem on Left
(B)
Cut 1

Double Leaf
(K)
Cut 2

Large Flower
(N)
Cut 2

Center Flower
(P)
Cut 4

Bud
(O)
Cut 1

Large Leaf
(I)
Cut 2 &
2 Reversed

Medium Leaf
(H)
Cut 8

Double Leaf
(J)
Cut 3

2nd From
Right Stem
(C)
Cut 1

Bottom Curved
Stem on Left
(E)
Cut 1

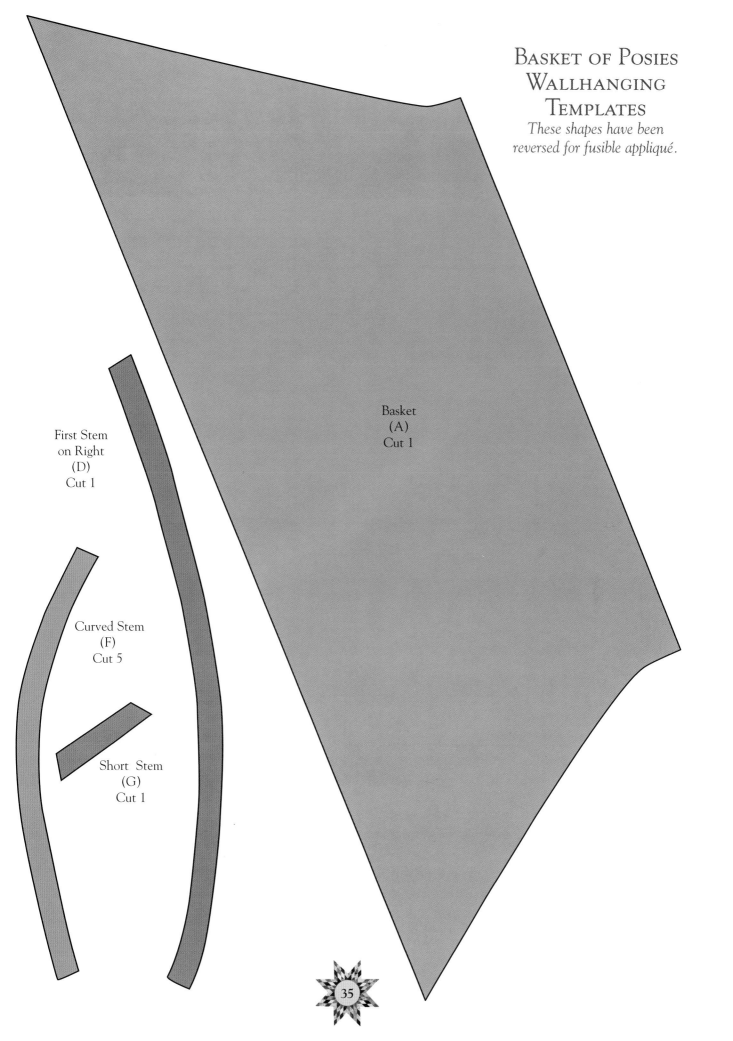

BASKET OF POSIES
WALLHANGING
TEMPLATES
*These shapes have been
reversed for fusible appliqué.*

Basket
(A)
Cut 1

First Stem
on Right
(D)
Cut 1

Curved Stem
(F)
Cut 5

Short Stem
(G)
Cut 1

Basket of Posies Wallhanging

Designed and pieced by Edyta Sitar for Laundry Basket Quilts

Gather seeds of knowledge everywhere
you go and your basket will
soon overflow with beautiful blossoms.

Blue Barn Quilt

Materials

- Variety of dark brown, blue, and rust 1-1/4"-wide print and batik strips (approximately 34 strips)
- Variety of medium blue, green, and gold 1-1/4"-wide print and batik strips (approximately 60 strips)
- Variety of light beige 1-1/4"-wide print and batik strips (approximately 75 strips)
- 3/4 yard dark batik for inner border and binding
- 1-1/4 yards dark print for outer border
- 7-1/4 yards backing fabric
- 86" square batting

Finished block: 6-3/4" square
Finished quilt: 80" square

Quantities are for 40/44"-wide, 100% cotton fabrics. Measurements include 1/4" seam allowances. Sew with right sides together unless otherwise stated.

Cut the Fabrics

From assorted dark 1-1/4"-wide print and batik strips, cut:

36 – 1-1/4" center squares (I selected rust for many of my center squares)
36 – 1-1/4" x 2" C logs
36 – 1-1/4" x 2-3/4" D logs
36 – 1-1/4" x 3-1/2" G logs
36 – 1-1/4" x 4-1/4" H logs
36 – 1-1/4" x 5" K logs
36 – 1-1/4" x 5-3/4" L logs
36 – 1-1/4" x 6-1/2" O logs
36 – 1-1/4" x 7-1/4" P logs

From assorted medium 1-1/4"-wide print and batik strips, cut:

64 – 1-1/4" center squares (I selected gold for many of my center squares)
64 – 1-1/4" x 2" C logs
64 – 1-1/4" x 2-3/4" D logs
64 – 1-1/4" x 3-1/2" G logs
64 – 1-1/4" x 4-1/4" H logs
64 – 1-1/4" x 5" K logs
64 – 1-1/4" x 5-3/4" L logs
64 – 1-1/4" x 6-1/2" O logs
64 – 1-1/4" x 7-1/4" P logs

From assorted light 1-1/4"-wide print and batik strips, cut:

100 – 1-1/4" square A logs
100 – 1-1/4" x 2" B logs
100 – 1-1/4" x 2-3/4" E logs
100 – 1-1/4" x 3-1/2" F logs
100 – 1-1/4" x 4-1/4" I logs
100 – 1-1/4" x 5" J logs
100 – 1-1/4" x 5-3/4" M logs
100 – 1-1/4" x 6-1/2" N logs

From dark batik, cut:

7 – 1-1/2" x 42" inner border strips
8 – 1-3/4" x 42" binding strips

From dark print, cut:

8 – 5-1/2" x 42" outer border strips

From backing, cut:

3 – 29-1/2" x 86" rectangles

Assemble the Log Cabin Blocks

1. Sew a light print or batik 1-1/4" square A log to a dark print or batik 1-1/4" center square. Press seam away from center square.

2. Sew a light print or batik 1-1/4" x 2" B log to the center square/A log from Step 1. Press seam toward B.

3. Continue adding the logs in a clockwise direction around the center square. Join logs in alphabetical order, using a pattern of two light logs followed by two dark logs as shown. Press seams away from the center after each log addition.

MAKE 36

4. Repeat Steps 1 - 3 to make a total of 36 dark/light log cabin blocks.

5. Repeat Steps 1 - 3, using medium print or batik logs in place of dark logs, to make a total of 64 medium/light log cabin blocks as shown.

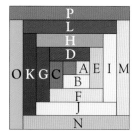

MAKE 64

ASSEMBLE THE QUILT CENTER

1. Referring to Quilt Center Assembly Diagram, lay out 36 dark/light log cabin blocks and 64 medium/light log cabin blocks in ten horizontal rows as shown.
2. Sew the blocks in each row together. Press seams in one direction, alternating the direction from row to row.
3. Join rows. Press seams in one direction.

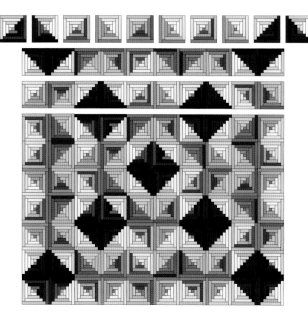

QUILT CENTER ASSEMBLY DIAGRAM

ADD THE BORDERS

1. Piece the 1-1/2" x 42" inner border strips to make the following: 2 – 1-1/2" x 68" for top and bottom and 2 – 1-1/2" x 70" for sides.
2. Referring to the Inner Border Diagram, sew the top and bottom inner border strips to the quilt

center. Press seams toward border. Sew the side inner border strips to the quilt center. Press seams toward border.

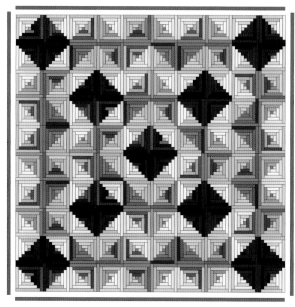

INNER BORDER DIAGRAM

3. Piece the 5-1/2" x 42" outer border strips to make the following: 2 – 5-1/2" x 70" for top and bottom and 2 – 5-1/2" x 80" for sides.
4. Referring to the Quilt Top Diagram, sew the top and bottom outer border strips to the quilt center. Press seams toward border. Sew the side outer border strips to the quilt center. Press seams toward border.

QUILT TOP DIAGRAM

Blue Barn Quilt

COMPLETE THE QUILT

1. Sew together the 29-1/2" x 86" backing rectangles along the long edges, using a 1/2" seam allowance. Press the seam allowance open.
2. Layer quilt top, batting, and pieced backing.

3. Quilt as desired. The quilt was stitched using neutral thread for an allover swirl pattern.
4. Bind with dark batik binding strips, referring to the Binding instructions on pages 12 - 13.

Designed and pieced by Edyta Sitar for Laundry Basket Quilts

Sewing Box

Materials

- Variety of medium-to-dark blue 7/8" to 1-3/8"-wide print and batik strips (approximately 12 strips)
- 2 – 1" x 11" medium-to-dark blue print or batik strips
- 2 – 11" x 4" rectangles of dark brown print for roof
- 2-1/2" x 5-1/4" rectangle of dark red print for door
- 2 – 2-3/4" squares of gold print or batik for windows
- 3/8 yard brown batik for bottom, binding, and ties
- 3/8 yard brown print for lining

Finished bag: 11" x 9-1/2" x 4-3/4"

Quantities are for 40/44"-wide, 100% cotton fabrics. Measurements include 1/4" seam allowances. Sew with right sides together unless otherwise noted.

NOTE: Refer to Strip Panels on pages 18 - 19 to sew together the 7/8" to 1-3/8"-wide print and batik strips to form two strip panels approximately 7-1/2" x 22". Press seams in one direction.

Cut the Fabrics

From the strip panels, cut:
1 – 11" x 6-1/4" back rectangle
2 – 4-3/4" x 6-1/4" side rectangles
2 – 4-3/4" x 3" front bottom rectangles
2 – 1-1/4" x 2-3/4" front center strips
2 – 1-3/4" x 2-3/4" front side rectangles

From brown batik, cut:
2 – 1-3/4" x 42" binding strips
4-3/4" x 11" bottom rectangle
1 – 1-1/2" x 15" tie strip

From brown print, cut:
1 – 11" x 23-1/4" lining rectangle
2 – 4-3/4" x 6-1/4" lining rectangles

Assemble the Bag Front

1. Sew 1-1/4" x 2-3/4" front center strips and 1-3/4" x 2-3/4" front side rectangles to opposite sides of the 2-3/4" gold print or batik window squares for window sections as shown. Press seams toward squares.

LEFT   RIGHT

2. Sew 4-3/4" x 3" front bottom rectangles to bottom edge of window sections. Press seams toward rectangles.

3. Sew together the window sections and the 2-1/2" x 5-1/4" dark red print door rectangle. Press seams toward door.

4. Sew two 1" x 11" medium-to-dark blue print or batik strips to the top of the house front and then a 11" x 4" dark brown print roof rectangle to complete the house front. Press seams toward strips.

5. Sew together the 11" x 6-1/4" strip panel back rectangle and the remaining 11" x 4" dark brown print roof rectangle to complete the house back. Press seams toward strips.

6. Join the house front and back with the 4-3/4" x 11" brown batik bottom rectangle. Press seams away from the bottom rectangle.

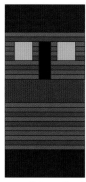

7. Sew the 4-3/4" x 6-1/4" strip panel side rectangles to the remaining edges of the brown batik bottom rectangle. Press seams toward side rectangles.

COMPLETE THE SEWING BAG

1. Center and sew the 4-3/4" x 6-1/4" lining rectangles on the long edges of the 11" x 23-1/4" lining rectangle as shown.

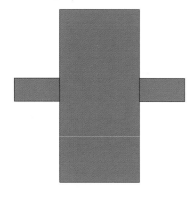

2. Use the assembled lining as a pattern to cut a piece of batting. Layer the pieced bag front, batting, and lining.

3. Quilt as desired. Neutral thread was used to stitch along the edges of the door, windows, and bag bottom. There is a 1" diagonal grid over the front and back roof and blue strips are stitched in-the-ditch.

4. Press under 3/8" on the long edges of the brown batik 1-1/2" x 15" tie strip. Fold strip in half lengthwise, aligning the pressed edges; press again. Sew the long edges together opposite the fold. Cut strip in half.

5. On the lining side of the bag, sew a tie centered on each top roof edge. Diagonally trim the loose ends of ties.

6. Bind the remaining short edges of the bag sides with brown batik binding strips.

7. With lining sides together, fold up one bag side along the bottom seam to align its raw edges with those of the bag front and back. Use a scant 1/4" seam to machine-baste the side to the front and back. Repeat on the opposite side of bag.

8. Bind all raw edges of bag with brown batik binding strips, referring to the Binding instructions on pages 12 - 13. Enclose the sewn tie ends in the binding.

Sewing Box
Designed and pieced by Edyta Sitar for Laundry Basket Quilts

Buttons, favorite threads, needles,
and pins can be tucked
safely away in a quilter's sewing box.

DOLL QUILT

Materials

- 1/8 yard or 9" x 22" (fat eighth) piece of cream print for block 1
- 1/8 yard or 9" x 22" (fat eighth) piece of navy print for block 1
- 1/3 yard total assorted light prints and batiks for block 2
- 1/3 yard total assorted medium to dark prints and batiks for block 2
- 1/4 yard beige print for border
- 1/8 yard dark print for binding
- 26" square backing fabric
- 26" square batting

Finished block: 5" square
Finished quilt: 19-1/2" square

Quantities are for 40/44"-wide, 100% cotton fabrics. Measurements include 1/4" seam allowances. Sew with right sides together unless otherwise stated.

NOTE: Follow the instructions given to make half-square triangles or refer to pages 16 - 17 for instructions on using Laundry Basket Quilts Half Square Triangle Exchange Paper.

CUT THE FABRICS

From cream print, cut:
4 – 1-3/4" x 3" rectangles
4 – 1-3/4" squares
From navy print, cut:
1 – 3" square
8 – 1-3/4" squares
From assorted light prints and batiks, cut:
64 – 2-1/8" squares
From assorted medium-to-dark prints and batiks, cut:
64 – 2-1/8" squares
From beige print, cut:
2 – 2-1/2" x 15-1/2" border strips
2 – 2-1/2" x 19-1/2" border strips
From dark print, cut:
2 – 1-3/4" x 42" binding strips

ASSEMBLE BLOCK 1

1. Draw a diagonal line across the wrong side of the eight navy print 1-3/4" squares.

2. Place a navy print 1-3/4" square on one end of a cream print 1-3/4" x 3" rectangle, right sides together as shown. Sew on the drawn line. Trim seam to 1/4" and press seams toward triangle.

3. Sew another navy print 1-3/4" square to the opposite end of the rectangle in the same manner to make a flying geese unit. Repeat Steps 2 - 3 to make a total of 4 flying geese units. The flying geese units should measure 1-3/4" x 3".

MAKE 4

4. Sew a flying geese unit to opposite edges of the navy print 3" square. Press seams toward the square.

5. Sew a cream print 1-3/4" square to each end of the remaining flying geese units. Press seams toward the squares. Sew these units to the remaining edges of the navy print 3" square to complete a block. Press seams toward the navy print square.

MAKE 2

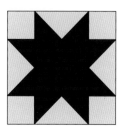
BLOCK 1
MAKE 1

Doll Quilt

Assemble Block 2

1. With right sides together, layer a light print or batik 2-1/8" square with a medium-to-dark print or batik 2-1/8" square. Draw a diagonal line across the wrong side of the light square.

2. Sew 1/4" on both sides of the drawn line. Cut apart on the drawn line. Press seam toward the dark triangle. The half-square triangles should measure 1-3/4" square. Repeat Steps 1 - 2 to make a total of 128 half-square triangles.

Make 128

3. Lay out 16 half-square triangles as shown.

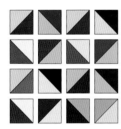

4. Sew the half-square triangles together in rows. Press the seams toward the dark triangles. Sew the rows together to complete one block 2; press. The block should measure 5-1/2" square. Repeat Steps 3 - 4 to make a total of 8 blocks.

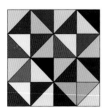

Block 2 Make 8

Assemble the Quilt Center

1. Referring to Quilt Center Assembly Diagram, lay out one Block 1 and eight Block 2 in three horizontal rows.
2. Sew the blocks in each row together. Press seams in one direction, alternating each row's direction. Join the rows to make the quilt center. Press seams in one direction. The quilt center should be 15-1/2" square.

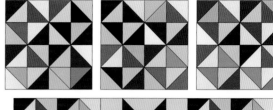

Quilt Center Assembly Diagram

Add the Border

1. Referring to the Quilt Top Assembly Diagram, sew 2-1/2" x 15-1/2" beige print border strips to opposite edges of the quilt center. Press seams toward the border.
2. Add 2-1/2" x 19-1/2" beige print border strips to remaining edges. Press seams toward border.

Quilt Top Assembly Diagram

Complete the Quilt

1. Layer quilt top, batting, and backing.
2. Quilt as desired. The quilt was stitched with a swirl pattern over the entire quilt top.
3. Bind with dark print binding strips, referring to the Binding instructions on pages 12 - 13.

Doll Quilt

Designed and pieced by Edyta Sitar for Laundry Basket Quilts

Egg Carton Quilt

Materials

- Variety of dark 1-1/2" x 21" print and batik strips (approximately 97 strips) for blocks and nine-patch units
- Variety of light 1-1/2" x 21" print and batik strips (approximately 74 strips) for blocks and nine-patch units
- 1-1/2 yards beige batik for blocks
- 1/8 yard gold print for center squares
- 1-1/2 yards blue-gray batik for sashing and hourglass units
- 1 yard total of assorted pink prints and batiks for hourglass units
- 3/4 yard brown print for inner border and binding
- 1/4 yard mauve batik for middle border
- 1-1/4 yards dark brown print for outer border
- 5 yards backing fabric
- 75" x 88" batting

Finished block: 10" square
Finished quilt: 68-1/2" x 81-1/2"

Quantities are for 40/44"-wide, 100% cotton fabrics. Measurements include 1/4" seam allowances. Sew with right sides together unless otherwise noted.

Cut the Fabrics

From beige batik, cut:
42 – 2" x 21" strips
80 – 2" squares
From gold print, cut:
20 – 1-1/2" squares
From blue-gray batik, cut:
49 – 3-1/2" x 4-1/2" rectangles
49 – 4-1/4" squares, cutting each diagonally in an X for a total of 196 triangles
From assorted pink prints and batiks, cut:
49 – 4-1/4" squares, cutting each diagonally in an X for a total of 196 triangles
From brown print cut:
6 – 1-1/2" x 42" inner border strips
8 – 1-3/4" x 42" binding strips
From mauve batik, cut:
7 – 1" x 42" middle border strips
From dark brown print, cut:
7 – 5-1/2" x 42" outer border strips
From backing, cut:
2 – 38" x 88" rectangles

Assemble the Block

1. Sew together three dark 1-1/2" x 21" print and batik strips, three light 1-1/2" x 21" print and batik strips and one beige 2" x 21" batik strip to make an A strip panel as shown. Press seams toward the dark strips. Repeat to make 7 A strip panels.

A Strip Panel
Make 7

2. Referring to the diagrams, sew together strips to make seven B, C, D, E, and F strip panels. Press seams toward the dark strips.

B Strip Panel
Make 7

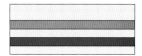

C Strip Panel
Make 7

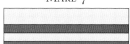

D Strip Panel
Make 7

E Strip Panel
Make 7

F Strip Panel
Make 7

3. Cut 1-1/2"-wide segments across the A strip panels as shown, cutting a total of 80 A segments. Repeat to cut 80 1-1/2"-wide segments each from the B, C, D, E, and F strip panels.

1-1/2"

4. Lay out a B, C, D, E, and F segment and one beige 2" batik square (G) as shown. Sew the segments and square together to complete one wedge. Press seams toward the B, D, and F segments. Repeat to make four wedges.

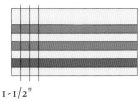

G F E D C B   MAKE 4

5. Lay out four wedges, four A segments, and one gold 1-1/2" print square as shown. Join the pieces together in rows. Press seams away from the A segments. Join the rows. Press seams away from the center.

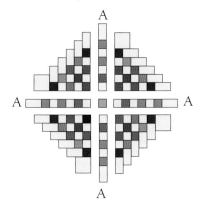

A

A   A

A

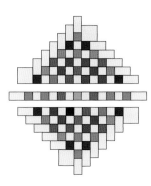

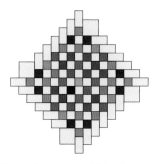

6. Place the pressed block on a cutting mat and use ruler and rotary cutter to center and trim to a 10-1/2" square.

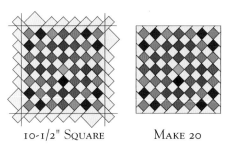

10-1/2" SQUARE   MAKE 20

7. Repeat Steps 4 - 6 to make a total of 20 blocks.

ASSEMBLE THE SASHING UNITS

1. Referring to the diagram, lay out two blue-gray batik triangles and two assorted pink triangles. Sew the triangles together in pairs. Press the seams toward the pink triangles. Join the pairs

together to make one hourglass unit. Press the seams in one direction. The pieced hourglass unit should measure 3-1/2" square. Repeat to make a total of 98 hourglass units.

MAKE 98

2. Add hourglass units to the ends of a blue-gray 3-1/2" x 4-1/2" rectangle to complete one sashing unit. Press seams toward rectangle. Repeat to make a total of 49 sashing units.

MAKE 49

MAKE THE NINE-PATCH UNITS

1. Sew together two dark 1-1/2" x 21" print or batik strips and one light 1-1/2" x 21" print or batik strip to make a dark/light/dark strip set as shown. Cut the strip set into 1-1/2"-wide segments. Make 5 dark/light/dark strip sets to cut 60 – 1-1/2"-wide segments.

1-1/2"

2. Sew together two light 1-1/2" x 21" print or batik strips and one dark 1-1/2" x 21" print or batik strip to make a light/dark/light strip set as shown. Cut the strip set into

Egg Carton Quilt

1-1/2"-wide segments. Make 3 light/dark/light strip sets to cut 30 – 1-1/2"-wide segments.

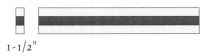

1-1/2"

3. Sew together two dark/light/dark segments and one light/dark/light segment to make a nine-patch unit as shown. Press seams in one direction. Repeat to make a total of 30 nine-patch units.

Make 30

Assemble the Quilt Center

1. Referring to the Quilt Center and Quilt Top Assembly Diagrams lay out the 20 blocks, 49 sashing units, and 30 nine-patch units in horizontal rows.

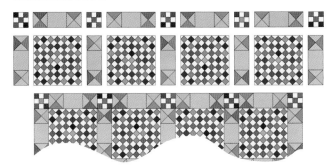

Quilt Center Assembly Diagram

2. Sew the pieces together in each row. Press the seam allowances toward the sashing units.

3. Join the rows to make the quilt center. Press seams in one direction.

Add the Borders

1. Piece the brown print 1-1/2" x 42" inner border strips to make the following: 2 – 1-1/2" x 68-1/2" for sides and 2 – 1-1/2" x 57" for top and bottom.

2. Referring to the Quilt Top Assembly Diagram, sew the side inner border strips to the quilt center. Press seams toward the border. Add the top and bottom inner border strips to the quilt center. Press seams toward the border.

3. Piece the mauve batik 1" x 42" middle border strips to make the following: 2 – 1" x 70-1/2" for sides and 2 – 1" x 58-1/2" for top and bottom.

4. Referring to the Quilt Top Assembly Diagram, sew the side middle border strips to the quilt top. Press seams toward the middle border. Add the top and bottom middle border strips to the quilt top. Press seams toward the middle border.

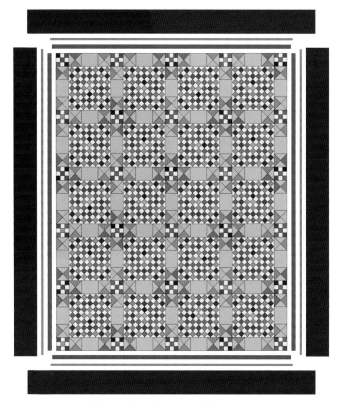

Quilt Top Assembly Diagram

5. Piece the dark brown print 5-1/2" x 42" strips to make the following: 2 – 5-1/2" x 71-1/2" for sides and 2 – 5-1/2" x 68-1/2" for top and bottom.

6. Referring to the Quilt Top Assembly Diagram, sew the side outer border strips to the quilt top. Press seams toward the outer border. Add the top and bottom outer border strips to the quilt top. Press seams toward the outer border.

Complete the Quilt

1. Sew the 38" x 88" backing rectangles along one long edge, using 1/2" seam allowance. Press the seam allowance open.

2. Layer quilt top, batting, and pieced backing.

3. Quilt as desired. The quilt was stitched using neutral thread for an allover wave pattern.

4. Bind with brown print binding strips, referring to the binding instructions on pages 12 - 13.

Egg Carton Quilt

Designed and pieced by Edyta Sitar for Laundry Basket Quilts

Pantry shelves lined with jars of delicious jams, jellies and honey tease our senses with the scrumptious smells of summer in the midst of winter.

CANDY NECKLACE QUILT

Materials

- Variety of light-to-dark 1"-1-1/2"-wide print and batik strips (approximately 96 strips) for strip panels
- 3-1/2 yards total assorted light prints for blocks and sashing
- Variety of dark 1-1/4" x 21" print and batik strips (approximately 65 strips) for blocks and nine-patch units
- Variety of light 1-1/4" x 21" print and batik strips (approximately 59 strips) for blocks and nine-patch units
- 16 – 1-1/4" squares of assorted dark print and batiks for block centers
- 1-1/3 yards beige print for border
- 1/2 yard dark print for binding
- 7-1/8 yards backing fabric
- 85" square batting

Finished block: 14-1/4" square
Finished quilt: 78-1/4" square

Quantities are for 40/44"-wide, 100% cotton fabrics. Measurements include 1/4" seam allowances. Sew with right sides together unless otherwise noted.

NOTE: Refer to Strip Panels on pages 18 - 19 to sew together the 1"-1-1/2"-wide print and batik strips to form a strip panel approximately 6" tall. Press seams in one direction. Make approximately 8 strip panels to cut 64 — 3-1/2" squares.

CUT THE FABRICS

From the strip panels, cut:
61 – 3-1/2" squares with the strips running diagonally across each square as shown
3 – 3-1/2" squares with the strips running across the width of each square as shown

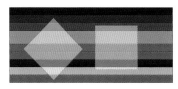

CUT 61   CUT 3

From assorted light prints, cut:
64 – 2-3/4" x 7-1/4" rectangles
40 – 2-3/4" x 14-3/4" sashing strips
128 – 2" x 2-3/4" rectangles
64 – 1-1/4" x 3-1/2" strips
From beige print, cut:
8 – 5-1/2" x 42" wide border strips
From dark print, cut:
8 – 1-3/4" x 42" binding strips
From backing, cut:
1 – 41" x 85" center rectangle
2 – 23" x 85" side rectangles

MAKE THE NINE-PATCH UNITS

1. Sew together two dark 1-1/4" x 21" print or batik strips and one light 1-1/4" x 21" print or batik strip to make a dark/light/dark strip set as shown. Press seams toward the dark strips. Make twelve dark/light/dark strip sets. Cut the strip sets into 178 – 1-1/4"-wide segments.

1-1/4"

MAKE 12   CUT 178

2. Sew together two light 1-1/4" x 21" print or batik strips and one dark 1-1/4" x 21" print or batik strip to make a light/dark/light strip set as shown. Press seams toward dark strip.

Make six light/dark/light strip sets. Cut the strip sets into 89 – 1-1/4"-wide segments.

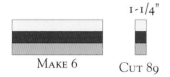

MAKE 6   CUT 89

1-1/4"

3. Sew together two dark/light/dark segments and one light/dark/light segment to make a nine-patch unit as shown. Press seams in one direction. Repeat to make a total of 89 nine-patch units.

MAKE 89

ASSEMBLE THE BLOCKS

1. Sew together the remaining 1-1/4" x 21" print and batik strips in pairs of one light and one dark to make 35 light/dark strip sets. Press seams toward dark strips.

MAKE 35

2. Cut a total of 128 – 3-1/2"-wide light/dark segments and 192 – 1-1/4"-wide light/dark segments from the 35 strip sets.

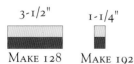

3-1/2"   1-1/4"

MAKE 128   MAKE 192

3. Sew together two 1-1/4"-wide light/dark segments, reversing the light and dark fabrics to make one four-patch unit. Press seam in one direction. Repeat to make 64 four-patch units. There will be 64 – 1-1/4"-wide segments remaining.

MAKE 64

4. Lay out four strip panel 3-1/2" squares, four light print 1-1/4" x 3-1/2" strips, and one dark print or batik 1-1/4" center square as shown. Sew the pieces together in rows. Press seams toward the light strips. Sew the rows together for the center section. Repeat to make 16 center sections.

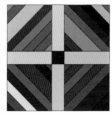

MAKE 16

5. Lay out one light print 2-3/4" x 7-1/4" rectangle, two light/dark 3-1/2"-wide segments, and one light/dark 1-1/4"-wide segment as shown. Sew the segments together. Press seams toward the center. Sew these to the light 2-3/4" x 7-1/4" rectangle to complete one side section. Repeat to make a total of 64 side sections.

MAKE 64

6. Lay out one nine-patch unit, one four-patch unit, and two light print 2" x 2-3/4" rectangles as shown. Sew the pieces together in rows. Press seams toward the rectangles.

Sew the rows together for one corner section. Repeat to make a total of 64 corner sections.

MAKE 64

7. Lay out one center section, four side sections, and four corner sections as shown.

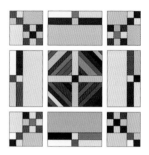

8. Sew the sections together in rows. Press the seams toward the side sections.

9. Sew the rows together to complete one block.

10. Repeat Steps 7 - 9 to make a total of 16 blocks.

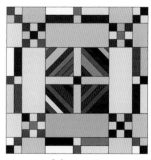

MAKE 16

Candy Necklace Quilt

ASSEMBLE THE QUILT CENTER

1. Referring to the Quilt Center Assembly Diagram, lay out 16 blocks, the 25 remaining nine-patch units, and 40 light 2-3/4" x 14-3/4" print or batik sashing strips as shown.
2. Sew the pieces together in rows. Press seams toward sashing strips.
3. Join the rows to make the quilt center. Press seams toward sashing rows.

ADD THE BORDER

1. Piece the beige print 5-1/2" x 42" border strips to make the following:
   2 – 5-1/2" x 66-3/4" for top and bottom and
   2 – 5-1/2" x 76-3/4" for sides.
2. Referring to the Quilt Top Assembly Diagram, sew the top and bottom border strips to the quilt center. Press seams toward the border. Sew the side border strips to the quilt center. Press seams toward the border.

COMPLETE THE QUILT

1. Sew the 23" x 85" side rectangles to the long edges of the 41" x 85" center rectangle, using a 1/2" seam allowance. Press the seam allowances of the backing open.
2. Layer quilt top, batting, and pieced backing.
3. Quilt as desired. The quilt was stitched using a floral pattern over the entire quilt top.
4. Bind with dark print binding strips, referring to the Binding instructions on pages 12 - 13.

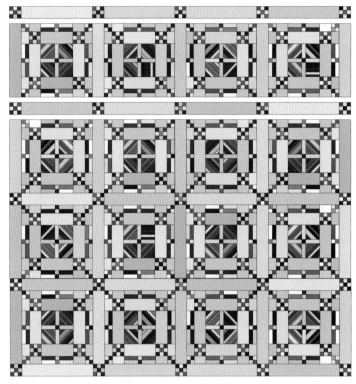

QUILT CENTER ASSEMBLY DIAGRAM

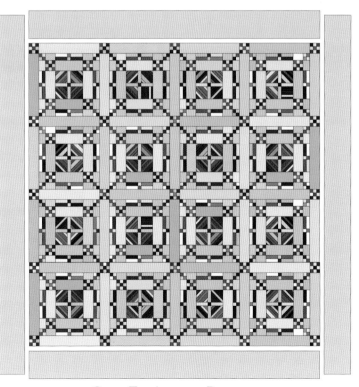

QUILT TOP ASSEMBLY DIAGRAM

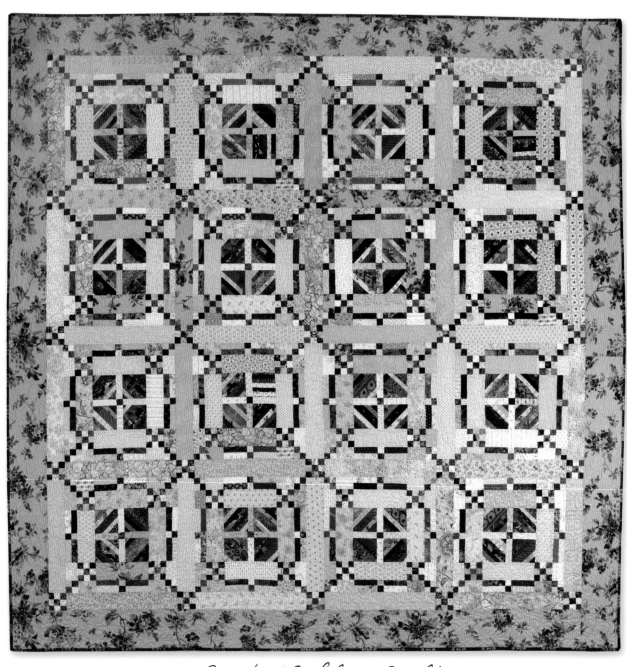

Candy Necklace Quilt
Designed and pieced by Edyta Sitar for Laundry Basket Quilts

What sweeter way to pass some time than sitting on your favorite candy-colored carousel horse, eating a favorite childhood treat.

MINI STAR QUILT

CUT THE FABRICS

From tan print, cut:
4 – 6" squares
1 – 8-3/4" square, cutting diagonally in an X for a total of 4 triangles
2 – 6" x 19" border strips
2 – 6" x 30" border strips
From dark plaid, cut:
4 – 1-3/4" x 42" binding strips

ASSEMBLE THE BLOCK

1. Sew together two light print or batik strips and two dark print or batik strips into a strip panel as shown, offsetting each strip by 1-1/4" and alternating the light and dark strips. Repeat to make four strip panels.

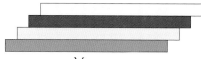

MAKE 4

2. Cut 1-1/2"-wide segments at a 45-degree angle across the strip panels as shown, cutting eight from each panel for a total of 32 segments.

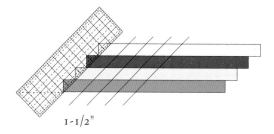

1-1/2"

3. Lay out four segments as shown. Sew the segments together to complete one diamond. Press seams in one direction. Repeat to make eight diamonds.

MAKE 8

Mini Star Quilt

4. Lay out the eight diamonds, four tan print 6"
   squares, and four tan print triangles as shown.
   Refer to 8-Pointed Star instructions on pages
   6 - 11 to complete the block.

ADD THE BORDER

1. Referring to the Quilt Top Assembly Diagram, sew
   6" x 19" border strips to opposite edges of the block.
   Press seams toward the border.
2. Add 6" x 30" border strips to the remaining edges.
   Press seams toward the border.

QUILT TOP ASSEMBLY DIAGRAM

APPLIQUÉ THE QUILT

1. Trace the appliqué patterns on page 66.
   Prepare the appliqué pieces using the instructions
   on pages 14 - 15 or the appliqué method of
   your choice.

**From assorted brown prints
and batiks, cut:**

4 of pattern A (long stem)

4 of pattern A reversed
   (long stem)

4 of pattern B (short stem)

4 of pattern B reversed
   (short stem)

From assorted green and blue prints and batiks, cut:

4 of pattern C (leaf)

4 of pattern C reversed (leaf)

4 of pattern D (leaf)

4 of pattern D reversed (leaf)

24 of pattern E (leaf)

8 of pattern F (leaf)

3 of pattern G (double leaf)

From gold prints and batiks, cut:

8 of pattern H (large flower)

8 of pattern I (small flower)

From pink prints and batiks, cut:

8 of pattern J (bud)

1 of pattern G (double leaf)

2. Position the appliqué pieces on the quilt top,
   referring to the Quilt Top Diagram as a guide.
   Appliqué the shapes in place using your favorite
   method. A narrow zigzag stitch was used along the
   edges of each of the appliqué pieces.

COMPLETE THE QUILT

1. Layer quilt top, batting, and backing.
2. Quilt as desired. Neutral thread was used to
   stitch closely around the appliqué shapes and
   in-the-ditch of the star's outer edges. The star is
   filled with stippling and the background is filled
   with an allover whimsical design.
3. Bind with dark plaid binding strips, referring to the
   Binding instructions on pages 12 - 13.

Mini Star Quilt

Quilt Top Diagram

MINI STAR QUILT TEMPLATES
These shapes have been reversed for fusible appliqué.

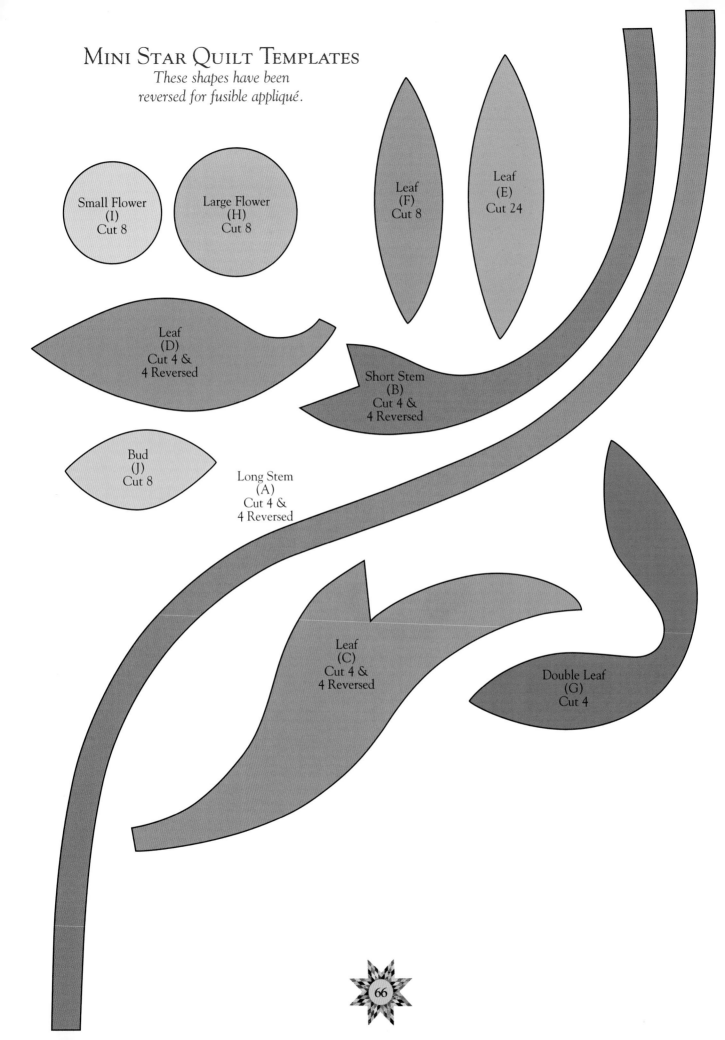

Small Flower
(I)
Cut 8

Large Flower
(H)
Cut 8

Leaf
(F)
Cut 8

Leaf
(E)
Cut 24

Leaf
(D)
Cut 4 &
4 Reversed

Short Stem
(B)
Cut 4 &
4 Reversed

Bud
(J)
Cut 8

Long Stem
(A)
Cut 4 &
4 Reversed

Leaf
(C)
Cut 4 &
4 Reversed

Double Leaf
(G)
Cut 4

Mini Star Quilt
Designed and pieced by Edyta Sitar for Laundry Basket Quilts

Sunset Star Quilt

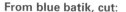

Materials

- 9 assorted 1-1/2" x 21" dark brown print and batik strips for blocks
- 18 assorted 1-1/2" x 21" medium-to-dark gold print and batik strips for blocks
- 27 assorted 1-1/2" x 21" medium-to-dark green print and batik strips for blocks
- 36 assorted 1-1/2" x 21" medium-to-dark blue print and batik strips for blocks
- 2 yards total assorted light beige prints and batiks for blocks and sashing
- 1/3 yard beige print for block corners
- Variety of 1-1/2" x width of fabric gold-to-brown print and batik strips for block border (approximately 18 strips)
- 1/8 yard or fat eighth blue batik for sashing squares
- 1-1/8 yards blue-brown batik for border
- 1/2 yard dark brown print for binding
- 4 yards backing fabric
- 69" square batting

Finished block: 15-1/2" square
Finished quilt: 63" square

Quantities are for 40/44"-wide, 100% cotton fabrics. Measurements include 1/4" seam allowances. Sew with right sides together unless otherwise noted.

Cut the Fabrics

NOTE: My finished block measures 15-1/2" square. Your block size may vary due to differences in piecing and trimming, so do not cut your block border strips and sashing strips until your blocks are completed. Adjust the length of your sashing and border strips if necessary.

From assorted light beige prints and batiks, cut:
45 – 1-3/4" x 21" strip panel strips
24 – 1-3/4" x 16" sashing strips

From beige print, cut:
18 – 4-5/8" squares, cutting each in half diagonally for a total of 36 corner triangles

From 1-1/2"-wide gold-to-brown print and batik strips, cut:
36 – 1-1/2" x 15" block border strips

From blue batik, cut:
16 – 1-3/4" sashing squares

From blue-brown batik, cut:
6 – 6" x 42" border strips

From dark brown print, cut:
7 – 1-3/4" x 42" binding strips

From backing, cut:
2 – 35" x 69" rectangles

Assemble the Blocks

NOTE: Numbers are used in the strip panel diagrams to indicate placement of the 1-1/2" x 21" and 1-3/4" x 21" strips. The strips' numbers are: 1 – brown, 2 – gold, 3 – green, 4 – blue, and 5 – light beige.

1. Sew together one each of strips 1 - 5 to complete an A strip panel as shown. Offset each strip by 1-1/4". Press seams toward the light beige strip.

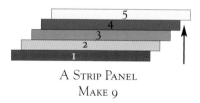

A Strip Panel
Make 9

2. Referring to the diagrams, sew together strips to make a B, C and D strip panel. Press seams in the direction indicated by the arrows.

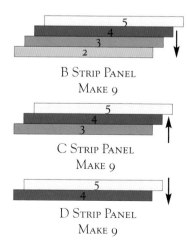

B Strip Panel
Make 9

C Strip Panel
Make 9

D Strip Panel
Make 9

3. Repeat Steps 1 and 2 to make a total of nine sets of strip panels A, B, C, and D. Use the remaining 1-3/4" x 21" light beige strips for the nine E strips.

4. Cut 1-1/2"-wide segments at a 45-degree angle across the A strip panels as shown. Cut eight from each panel for a total of 72 segments. Repeat to cut 72 segments each from the B, C, and D strip panels and E strips.

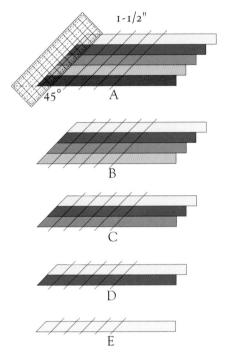

5. Lay out an A, B, C, D, and E segment as shown. Sew the segments together to complete one wedge. Press seams toward E. Repeat to make eight wedges.

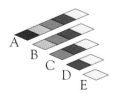

MAKE 8

6. Sew the wedges together in pairs. Make (4) pairs. Press seams as indicated by the arrow. Join the pairs to make two halves, carefully aligning the diamond seams. Trim "bunny ears" before pressing seams as indicated by the arrows.

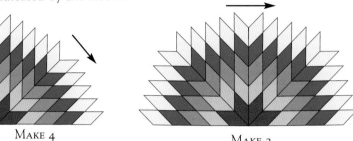

MAKE 4   MAKE 2

7. To join the two halves, begin sewing at the center of the star out to one edge and then again from the center out to the opposite edge. Press seam in a clockwise direction as shown by the arrows.

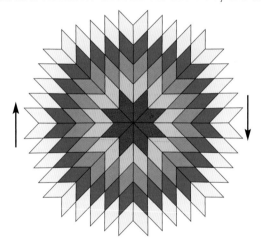

8. Place the pressed star on a cutting mat and use a ruler and rotary cutter to square up the four sides as shown. Be sure to leave at least 1/4" beyond the blue diamonds.

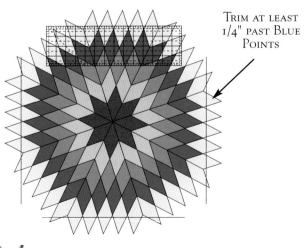

TRIM AT LEAST 1/4" PAST BLUE POINTS

9. Sew a beige corner triangle to one of the trimmed edges, aligning the middle of the triangle with the center of the trimmed edge. Repeat for each corner.

CENTER
TRIANGLE ON
TRIMMED EDGE

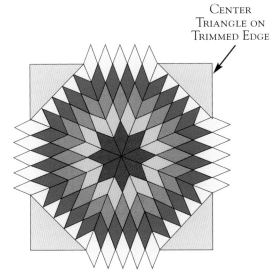

10. Repeat Steps 5 - 9 to make nine block centers. When all the block centers are complete, trim off the remaining points and square them all to the same size.
NOTE: My blocks were trimmed to 14" x 14", but your blocks may vary due to differences in piecing.

11. Sew one gold-to-brown 1-1/2" x 15" block border strip to the top edge of a block center, beginning at the left edge and stopping about 2" from the right edge. Press seam toward border strip.

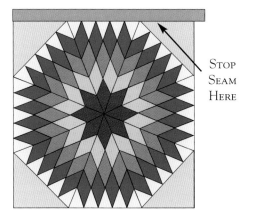

STOP
SEAM
HERE

12. Continue adding border strips in a counter-clockwise direction to the block center as shown. Press seams toward the border strips.

13. Sew the final border strip to the block center and press. Finish sewing the partial seam at the top edge to connect the borders, completing one block.

MAKE 9

Sunset Star Quilt

14. Repeat Steps 11 - 13 to add borders to each block center. Make nine blocks.

ASSEMBLE THE QUILT CENTER

1. Referring to the Quilt Center Assembly Diagram, lay out 9 blocks, 24 light beige 1-3/4" x 16" sashing strips, and 16 blue batik 1-3/4" sashing squares.

2. Sew the pieces together in each sashing/sashing square row and each block/sashing row. Press the seams toward the sashing strips.

3. Join the rows to make the quilt center. Press seams in one direction.

ADD THE BORDER

1. Piece the blue-brown batik 6" x 42" border strips to make the following: 2 – 6" x 52" side border strips and 2 – 6" x 63" top and bottom border strips.

2. Referring to the Quilt Top Assembly Diagram, sew the side border strips to the quilt center. Press seams toward border. Sew the top and bottom border strips to the quilt center. Press seams toward border.

COMPLETE THE QUILT

1. Sew the 35" x 69" backing rectangles along one long edge, using 1/2" seam allowance. Press the seam allowance open.

2. Layer quilt top, batting, and pieced backing.

3. Quilt as desired. The quilt was stitched using neutral thread for an allover swirl pattern.

4. Bind with dark brown print binding strips, referring to the binding instructions on pages 12 - 13.

QUILT CENTER ASSEMBLY DIAGRAM

QUILT TOP ASSEMBLY DIAGRAM

Sunset Star Quilt

Designed and pieced by Edyta Sitar for Laundry Basket Quilts

Sunshine Box Quilt

Materials

- 188 assorted light-to-dark 5" squares of print and batik fabrics
  (Charm fabric packs are perfect for this quilt
- 2 yards yellow fabric
- 1/2 yard dark print for binding
- 3-3/8 yards backing fabric
- 59" x 72" batting

Finished quilt: 52-1/2" x 65-1/2"

Quantities are for 40/44"-wide, 100% cotton fabrics. Measurements include 1/4" seam allowances. Sew with right sides together unless otherwise stated.

Cut the Fabrics

From assorted light-to-dark print and batik squares, cut:
188 hexagons using template A on page 76
From yellow fabric, cut:
364 triangles using template B on page 76
From dark print, cut:
7 – 1-3/4" x 42" binding strips
From backing, cut:
2 – 36-1/2" x 59" rectangles

Assemble the Quilt Top

1. Sew 2 triangles to opposite edges of a hexagon. Press seams toward hexagon. Repeat to make 176 hexagon/triangles.

MAKE 176

2. Sew 1 triangle to one edge of each of the 12 remaining hexagons; press seams toward the hexagons.

MAKE 12

3. Referring to the Quilt Top Assembly Diagram, lay out the 176 hexagon/triangles from Step 1 in 13 horizontal rows, using 14 in the 7 A rows and 13 in the 6 B rows. Add the 12 hexagons from Step 2 to the ends of the B rows as shown.

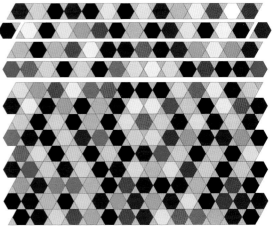

QUILT TOP ASSEMBLY DIAGRAM

4. Sew together the pieces in each row. Press seams in one direction, alternating the direction from row to row.
5. Join rows. Press seams in one direction.

Complete the Quilt

1. Sew together the 36-1/2" x 59" backing rectangles along the long edges, using a 1/2" seam allowance. Press the seam allowance open.
2. Layer quilt top, batting, and pieced backing.
3. Quilt as desired. The quilt was stitched with neutral thread and an allover swirl pattern.
4. Trim each end of the B rows on the diagonal 1/4" beyond the points of the last hexagon as shown.

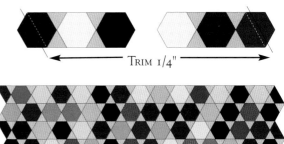

TRIM 1/4"

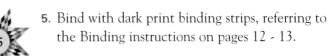

5. Bind with dark print binding strips, referring to the Binding instructions on pages 12 - 13.

Sunshine Box Quilt

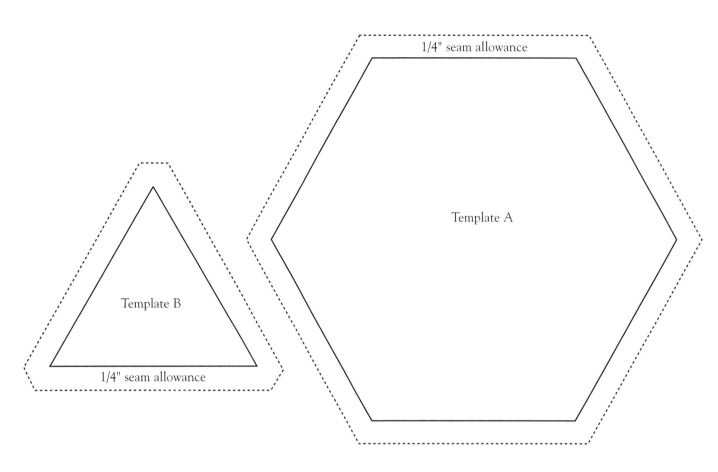

Template B

1/4" seam allowance

Template A

1/4" seam allowance

Sunshine Box Quilt

Designed and pieced by Edyta Sitar for Laundry Basket Quilts

BUSHEL BASKET QUILT

Materials

- 18 assorted medium-to-dark 3" print and batik squares for block centers
- 5/8 yard total assorted medium-to-dark prints and batiks for block centers
- Variety of 1"-wide print and batik strips (approximately 140 strips for blocks and 85 strips for border)
- Variety of 1-1/2"-wide print and batik strips (approximately 12 strips) for border
- 1/2 yard black print for binding
- 4-1/8 yards backing fabric
- 73" square batting

    Finished block: 4-1/2" square
    Finished quilt: 66-1/2" square

    Quantities are for 40/44"-wide, 100% cotton fabrics. Measurements include 1/4" seam allowances. Sew with right sides together unless otherwise stated.

    NOTE: Refer to Strip Panels on pages 18 - 19 to sew together the 1" and 1-1/2"-wide print and batik strips to form a strip panel approximately 18" x 40"-44". Press seams in one direction. Make approximately 3 strip panels to cut enough 6-1/2"-wide segments to make two 6-1/2" x 54-1/2" border strips and two 6-1/2" x 66-1/2" border strips.

CUT THE FABRICS

From the fabric strip panels, cut:

6-1/2"-wide segments, no more than 18"-tall, to make two 6-1/2" x 54-1/2" and two 6-1/2" x 66-1/2" pieced border strips

From assorted medium-to-dark prints and batiks, cut:

126 – 2" center squares

NOTE: Cut the 1"-wide print and batik strips in sets of four matching strips for the blocks. Each Block 1 needs three sets of four matching strips; two each of A and B, two each of C and D, and two each of E and F. Each Block 2 needs two sets of four matching strips; two each of C and D and two each of E and F.

From assorted 1"-wide print and batik strips, cut:

252 – 1" x 2" A strips
252 – 1" x 3" B strips
288 – 1" x 3" C strips
288 – 1" x 4" D strips
288 – 1" x 4" E strips
288 – 1" x 5" F strips

From black print, cut:

7 – 1-3/4"-wide binding strips

From backing, cut:

2 – 37" x 73" rectangles

ASSEMBLE BLOCK 1

1. Sew matching print or batik 1" x 2" A strips to opposite edges of a medium-to-dark print or batik 2" center square. Press seams away from center square. Sew matching 1" x 3" B strips to the remaining edges of the center square. Press seams away from center square.

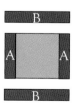

2. Sew matching print or batik 1" x 3" C strips to opposite edges of the block. Press seams away from the center. Sew matching 1" x 4" D strips to the remaining edges of the block. Press seams away from the center.

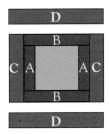

3. Sew matching print or batik 1" x 4" E strips to opposite edges of the block. Press seams away from the center. Sew matching 1" x 5" F strips to the remaining edges to complete the block. Press seams away from the center.

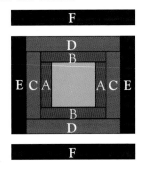

4. Repeat Steps 1 - 3 to make a total of 126 Block 1.

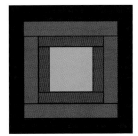

BLOCK 1
MAKE 126

ASSEMBLE BLOCK 2

1. Sew matching print or batik 1" x 3" C strips to opposite edges of a medium-to-dark print or batik 3" center square. Press seams away from the center square. Sew matching 1" x 4" D strips to the remaining edges of the center square. Press seams away from the center.

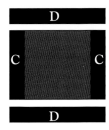

2. Sew matching print or batik 1" x 4" E strips to opposite edges of the block. Press seams away from the center. Sew matching 1" x 5" F strips to the remaining edges to complete one block. Press seams away from the center.

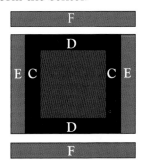

3. Repeat Steps 1 - 2 to make a total of 18 Block 2.

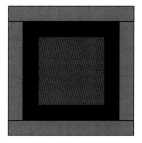

BLOCK 2
MAKE 18

ASSEMBLE THE QUILT CENTER

1. Refer to the Quilt Center Assembly Diagram on page 81 to lay out 126 Block 1 and 18 Block 2 in 12 horizontal rows of 12 blocks, positioning Block 2 randomly in the rows.

2. Sew the blocks in each row together. Press seams in one direction, alternating direction from row to row.

3. Join rows. Press seams in one direction.

Bushel Basket Quilt

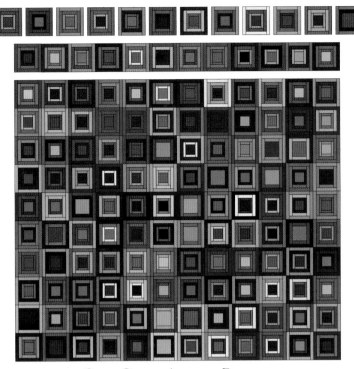

QUILT CENTER ASSEMBLY DIAGRAM

ADD THE BORDER

1. Lay out enough 6-1/2"-wide segments to create a 54-1/2"-long side border. Sew the segments together; press seams in one direction. Repeat to make another 54-1/2"-long side border and two 66-1/2"-long top and bottom borders.

2. Measure to check the length of the pieced borders. If necessary, make minor adjustments to some seams to adjust the length so two measure 54-1/2"-long and two measure 66-1/2"-long.

3. Referring to the Quilt Top Assembly Diagram, sew side border strips to the quilt center. Press seams toward the quilt center. Add the top and bottom border strips to the quilt center. Press seams toward the quilt center.

COMPLETE THE QUILT

1. Sew together the 37" x 73" backing rectangles along one long edge, using a 1/2" seam allowance. Press the seam allowance open.

2. Layer quilt top, batting, and pieced backing.

3. Quilt as desired. The quilt was stitched using neutral thread for an allover rainbow pattern.

4. Bind with black print binding strips, referring to the Binding instructions on pages 12 - 13.

QUILT TOP ASSEMBLY DIAGRAM

Bushel Basket Quilt

Designed and pieced by Edyta Sitar for Laundry Basket Quilts

A countryside picnic should always
include a favorite quilt and a picnic basket full
of the season's sweetest, freshest produce.

Swan Lake Quilt

Materials

- 3 yards beige batik for appliqué foundations and half-square triangles
- 5/8 yard beige-and-black batik for inner border
- 1 yard total of assorted dark prints and batiks for inner border
- 1 yard black print for outer border
- 1/2 yard brown batik for binding
- 9 – 5" squares of assorted dark pink and red prints and batiks for large flower appliqués
- 9 – 4" squares of assorted pink prints and batiks for small flower appliqués
- 9 – 4" squares of assorted yellow and gold prints and batiks for flower center appliqués
- 9 – 10" squares of assorted green prints and batiks for double leaf appliqués
- 9 – 4" x 6" rectangles of assorted green, blue, and brown prints and batiks for single leaf appliqués
- 9 – 4" x 12" rectangles of assorted dark prints and batiks for stem appliqués
- 9 – 6" squares of assorted dark prints and batiks for rounded-corner appliqués
- 9 – 4" squares of assorted dark prints and batiks for spoke appliqués
- 4-1/8 yards backing fabric
- 73" square batting

Finished block: 16" square
Finished quilt: 66-1/2" square

Quantities are for 40/44"-wide, 100% cotton fabrics. Measurements include 1/4" seam allowances. Sew with right sides together unless otherwise noted.

Cut the Fabrics

From beige batik, cut:
9 – 20" foundation squares
70 – 2-1/4" squares
From beige-and-black batik, cut:
6 – 9-1/4" squares, cutting each diagonally in an X for a total of 24 triangles
From assorted dark prints and batiks, cut:
7 – 5-1/4" squares, cutting each diagonally in an X for a total of 28 large triangles
14 – 3-1/4" squares, cutting each diagonally in an X for a total of 56 small triangles
70 – 2-1/4" squares
From black print, cut:
6 – 5-1/2" x 42" outer border strips
From brown batik, cut:
7 – 1-3/4" x 42" binding strips
From backing, cut:
2 – 37" x 73" rectangles

Cut and Assemble the Appliqué Blocks

1. Trace the appliqué patterns on page 88. Prepare the appliqué pieces using the instructions on pages 14 - 15 or the appliqué method of your choice.

From *each* 5" dark pink and red print or batik square, cut:
4 of pattern A (large flower) for a total of 36
From *each* 4" pink print and batik square, cut:
4 of pattern B (small flower) for a total of 36
From *each* 4" yellow and gold print batik square, cut:
4 of pattern C (flower center) for a total of 36
From *each* 10" green print and batik square, cut:
8 of pattern D (double leaf) for a total of 72
From *each* 4" x 6" assorted print and batik rectangle, cut:
4 of pattern E (single leaf) for a total of 36
From *each* 4" x 12" assorted dark print and batik rectangle, cut:
4 of pattern F (stem) for a total of 36, then from *each* F cut one 5-1/4" stem and one 4" stem
From *each* 6" assorted dark print and batik square, cut:
4 of pattern G (rounded-corner) for a total of 36
From *each* 4" assorted dark print and batik square, cut:
1 of pattern H (spoke) for a total of 9

2. Position one set of appliqué pieces on each 20" beige batik foundation square, referring to the Appliqué Placement Diagram on page 89. Appliqué the shapes in place using your favorite method. Press appliquéd blocks from the back. Center and trim each to a 16-1/2" square.

MAKE 9

NOTE: The fabric for the appliqués in the Swan Lake Quilt vary from block to block, sometimes using all the same fabric on one block for a leaf or flower shape and sometimes using up to four different fabrics for the same shape.

ASSEMBLE THE QUILT CENTER

1. Lay out nine blocks in three rows, referring to the Quilt Center Assembly Diagram.

QUILT CENTER ASSEMBLY DIAGRAM

2. Sew the blocks in each row together. Press seams in one direction, alternating direction from row to row.

3. Join rows to make the quilt center. Press seams in one direction.

ADD THE BORDERS

1. With right sides together, layer a beige batik 2-1/4" square with a dark print or batik 2-1/4" square. Draw a diagonal line across the wrong side of the beige batik square.

2. Sew 1/4" on both sides of the drawn line. Cut apart on the drawn line. Press seams toward the dark triangle. The half-square triangles should measure 1-7/8" square. Repeat Steps 1 - 2 to make a total of 140 half-square triangles.

MAKE 140

3. Sew half-square triangles together in one row of two and one row of three referring to the diagram for placement of half-square triangles. Press seams in one direction. Add a dark print or batik small triangle to each piece for left and right side sections.

LEFT SIDE   RIGHT SIDE

4. Sew the left side section to a dark print or batik large triangle. Press seams toward the large triangle. Sew the right side section to the large triangle to complete one pieced triangle; press seams toward the large triangle. Repeat Steps 3 - 4 to make a total of 28 pieced triangles.

MAKE 28

5. Sew together five pieced triangles from Step 4 and six beige-and-black batik triangles in a row as shown. Press seams toward beige-and-black batik triangles. Repeat to make four inner borders.

MAKE 4

6. Referring to Inner Border Diagram, sew an inner border row to each edge of the quilt center. Press seams toward the quilt center.

7. Sew together the remaining pieced triangles in pairs. Press seams in one direction. Add a pair to each corner of the quilt center.

8. Piece the 5-1/2" x 42" outer border strips to make the following: 2 – 5-1/2" x 56-1/2" for top and bottom and 2 – 5-1/2" x 66-1/2" for sides.

9. Referring to the Quilt Top Assembly Diagram, sew 5-1/2" x 56-1/2" top and bottom outer border strips to the quilt center. Press seams toward outer border.

10. Sew 5-1/2" x 66-1/2" side outer border strips to the remaining edges. Press seams toward outer border.

COMPLETE THE QUILT

1. Sew together the 37" x 73" backing rectangles along one long edge, using a 1/2" seam allowance. Press the seam allowance open.

2. Layer quilt top, batting, and pieced backing.

3. Quilt as desired. The quilt was stitched closely around the appliqué shapes and in-the-ditch of the small dark triangles in the inner border. A feathered vine was added in the outer border that overlaps the large dark triangles in the inner border. An allover whimsical design was used to fill in the background of the blocks and the light colored areas of the inner border.

4. Bind with brown batik binding strips, referring to the Binding instructions on pages 12 - 13.

INNER BORDER DIAGRAM

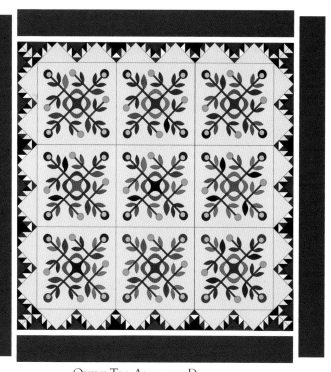

QUILT TOP ASSEMBLY DIAGRAM

SWAN LAKE QUILT TEMPLATES
These shapes have been reversed for fusible appliqué.

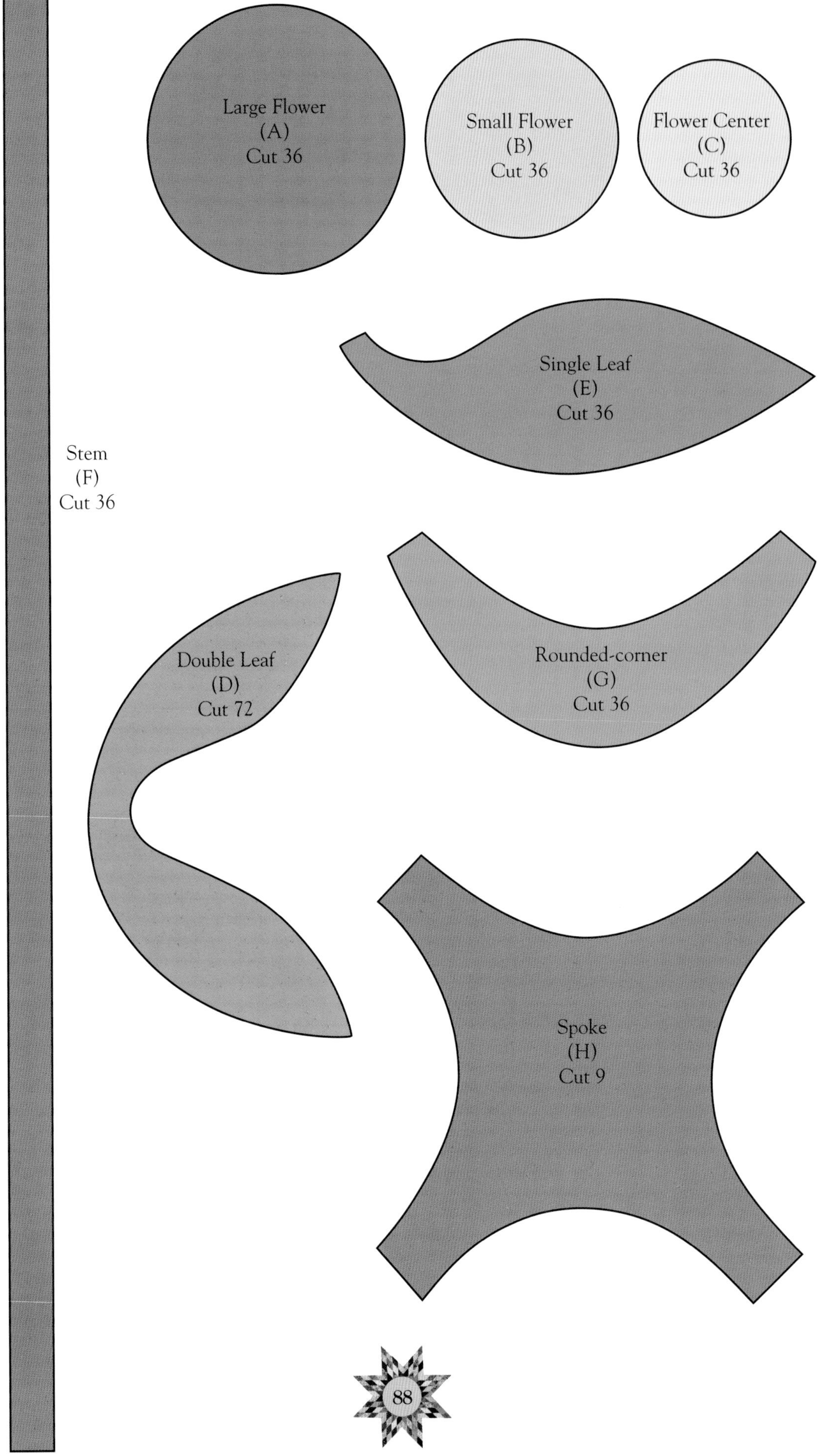

Large Flower
(A)
Cut 36

Small Flower
(B)
Cut 36

Flower Center
(C)
Cut 36

Single Leaf
(E)
Cut 36

Stem
(F)
Cut 36

Double Leaf
(D)
Cut 72

Rounded-corner
(G)
Cut 36

Spoke
(H)
Cut 9

Swan Lake Appliqué Placement Diagram

Swan Lake Quilt

Designed and pieced by Edyta Sitar for Laundry Basket Quilts

Collectibles and treasures like these Amish bonnets were found in a quaint shop in Shipshewana, conjuring up simpler times still followed by the Amish community.

COBBLESTONES QUILT

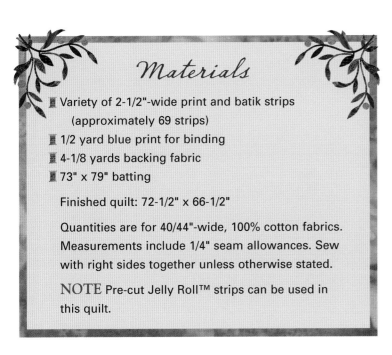

Materials

- Variety of 2-1/2"-wide print and batik strips (approximately 69 strips)
- 1/2 yard blue print for binding
- 4-1/8 yards backing fabric
- 73" x 79" batting

Finished quilt: 72-1/2" x 66-1/2"

Quantities are for 40/44"-wide, 100% cotton fabrics. Measurements include 1/4" seam allowances. Sew with right sides together unless otherwise stated.

NOTE Pre-cut Jelly Roll™ strips can be used in this quilt.

CUT THE FABRICS

From assorted 2-1/2"-wide print and batik strips, cut:
545 – 2-1/2" x 5" rectangles
From blue print, cut:
7 – 1-3/4" x 42" binding strips
From backing, cut:
2 – 40" x 73" rectangles

ASSEMBLE THE QUILT TOP

1. Referring to the Quilt Top Assembly Diagram on page 94, lay out the 545 rectangles in 33 horizontal rows. Use 17 rectangles in the 17 A rows and 16 rectangles in the 16 B rows. Center the B rows under the A rows. Begin with an A row at the middle of the quilt and start with a single dark brown rectangle at the center of that row. Working outward from the center dark brown rectangle, add brown rectangles around it, followed by golds, creams and pinks-to-reds.

2. Continue adding rectangles in browns, and blues around the center. Randomly place the remaining rectangles to complete the 33 rows.

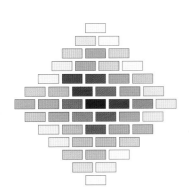

QUILT CENTER BROWNS TO CREAMS

QUILT CENTER PINKS-TO-REDS, BROWNS, AND BLUES

Cobblestones Quilt

NOTE: The rectangles at the ends of the A rows extend beyond the B rows and will be trimmed later.

3. Sew together the rectangles in each row. Press seams in one direction.

4. Join rows. Press seams in one direction.

COMPLETE THE QUILT

1. Trim the left and right edges of the quilt top as shown in the Quilt Top Assembly Diagram.

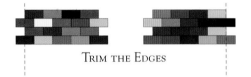

TRIM THE EDGES

2. Sew together the 40" x 73" backing rectangles along the long edges, using a 1/2" seam allowance. Press the seam allowance open.

3. Layer quilt top, batting, and pieced backing.

4. Quilt as desired. The quilt was stitched with neutral thread and an allover rainbow pattern.

5. Bind with blue print binding strips, referring to the Binding instructions on pages 12 - 13.

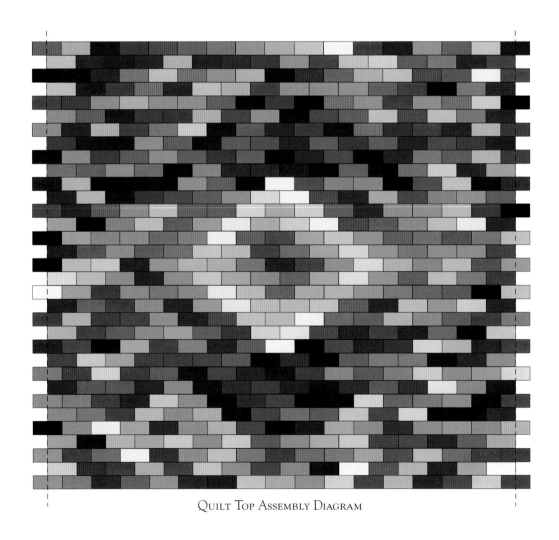

QUILT TOP ASSEMBLY DIAGRAM

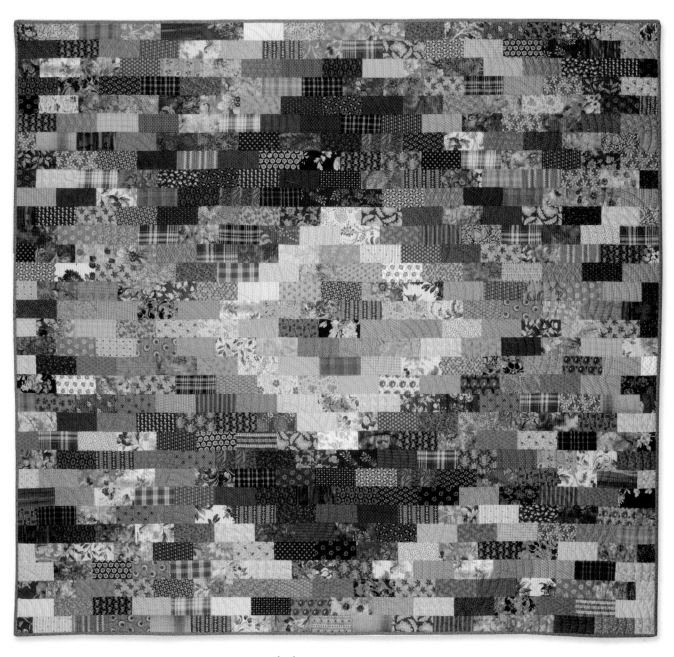

Cobblestones Quilt

Designed and pieced by Edyta Sitar for Laundry Basket Quilts

BLUEBERRY FARM QUILT

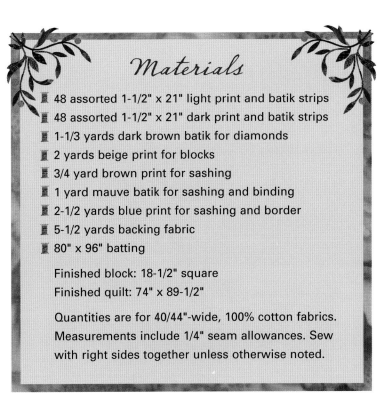

Materials

- 48 assorted 1-1/2" x 21" light print and batik strips
- 48 assorted 1-1/2" x 21" dark print and batik strips
- 1-1/3 yards dark brown batik for diamonds
- 2 yards beige print for blocks
- 3/4 yard brown print for sashing
- 1 yard mauve batik for sashing and binding
- 2-1/2 yards blue print for sashing and border
- 5-1/2 yards backing fabric
- 80" x 96" batting

Finished block: 18-1/2" square
Finished quilt: 74" x 89-1/2"

Quantities are for 40/44"-wide, 100% cotton fabrics. Measurements include 1/4" seam allowances. Sew with right sides together unless otherwise noted.

CUT THE FABRICS

From dark brown batik, cut:
10 – 4-1/2" x 42" strips; cut a total of 48
    4-1/2" diamonds from the strips
    (see Cutting Diamonds)

From beige print, cut:
48 – 6" squares
12 – 8-3/4" squares, cutting each diagonally
    in an X for a total of 48 triangles

From dark brown print, cut:
30 – 1-1/2" x 19" sashing strips

From mauve batik, cut:
15 – 1-1/2" x 19" sashing strips
8 – 1-3/4" x 42" binding strips

From blue print, cut:
2 – 3-1/2" x 89-1/2" vertical
    sashing strips
2 – 6-1/2" x 89-1/2" vertical
    border strips

From backing, cut:
2 – 40-1/2" x 96" rectangles

CUTTING DIAMONDS

Trim end of a 4-1/2"-wide dark brown batik strip at a 45-degree angle. Place the 4-1/2" line of ruler along the angled edge of the strip. Cut along edge of ruler to make one diamond. Continue in this manner to cut a total of 48 diamonds from the 10 strips.

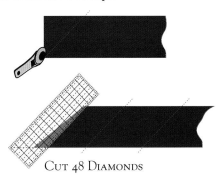

CUT 48 DIAMONDS

ASSEMBLE THE BLOCK

1. Sew together two light 1-1/2" x 21" and two dark 1-1/2" x 21" strips into a strip panel as shown, offsetting each strip by 1-1/4" and alternating the light and dark strips. Repeat to make 24 strip panels.

MAKE 24

2. Cut 1-1/2"-wide segments at a 45-degree angle across the strip panels as shown, cutting eight from each panel for a total of 192 segments.

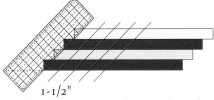

1-1/2"

3. Lay out four segments as shown. Sew the segments together to complete one pieced diamond. Press seams in one direction. Repeat to make 48 pieced diamonds.

MAKE 48

Blueberry Farm Quilt

4. Lay out four pieced diamonds, four dark brown batik diamonds, four beige print 6" squares, and four beige print triangles as shown. Refer to 8-Pointed Star instructions on pages 6 - 11 to complete the block. Repeat to make 12 blocks.

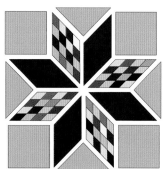

MAKE 12

ASSEMBLE THE QUILT TOP

1. Sew two dark brown print 1-1/2" x 19" sashing strips and one mauve batik 1-1/2" x 19"sashing strip together as shown to make a horizontal sashing strip. Press seams toward mauve strip. Repeat to make 15 horizontal sashing strips.

MAKE 15

2. Lay out four blocks and five horizontal sashing strips to create a vertical row. Sew the pieces together; press seams toward sashing. Repeat to make a total of three rows.

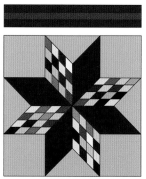

MAKE 3

98

Blueberry Farm Quilt

3. Referring to the Quilt Top Assembly Diagram, sew the blue print 3-1/2" x 89-1/2" vertical sashing strips to the long edges of the center block row. Sew the two remaining block rows to the opposite long edges of the vertical sashing strips to complete the quilt center. Press all seams toward sashing strips.

4. Sew the blue print 6-1/2" x 89-1/2" border strips to the left and right edges of the quilt center. Press seams toward border.

COMPLETE THE QUILT

1. Sew together the 40-1/2" x 96" backing rectangles along one long edge, using a 1/2" seam allowance. Press the seam allowance open.

2. Layer quilt top, batting, and pieced backing.

3. Quilt as desired. A neutral thread was used to stitch a swirl pattern over the blocks and horizontal sashing and a cable design in the vertical sashing strips and border.

4. Bind with mauve batik binding strips, referring to the Binding instructions on pages 12 - 13.

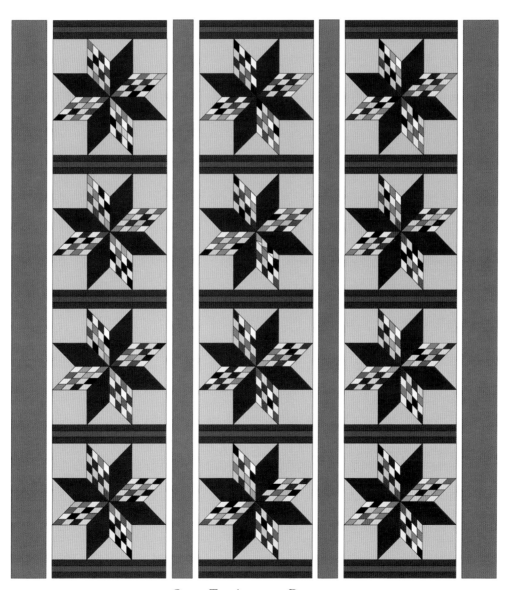

QUILT TOP ASSEMBLY DIAGRAM

Blueberry Farm Quilt
Designed and pieced by Edyta Sitar for Laundry Basket Quilts

An open gate is a welcome sign for travelers to stop and enjoy fresh blueberries. All will leave with a new appreciation for the simple life, as well as blue fingertips and a tummy full of summer's goodness.

Lil' Baskets Quilt

Materials

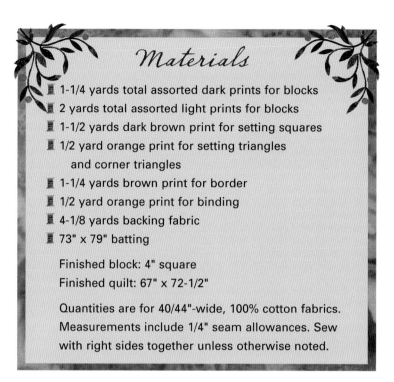

- 1-1/4 yards total assorted dark prints for blocks
- 2 yards total assorted light prints for blocks
- 1-1/2 yards dark brown print for setting squares
- 1/2 yard orange print for setting triangles and corner triangles
- 1-1/4 yards brown print for border
- 1/2 yard orange print for binding
- 4-1/8 yards backing fabric
- 73" x 79" batting

Finished block: 4" square
Finished quilt: 67" x 72-1/2"

Quantities are for 40/44"-wide, 100% cotton fabrics. Measurements include 1/4" seam allowances. Sew with right sides together unless otherwise noted.

Cut the Fabrics

NOTE: Most blocks were assembled using one large and two small matching triangles for the basket and four matching half-square triangles. The other block pieces are cut from a variety of light print fabrics for a very scrappy look.

From assorted dark prints, cut:

55 – 2-7/8" squares, cutting each in half diagonally for a total of 110 large triangles

110 – 1-7/8" squares, cutting each in half diagonally for a total of 220 small triangles

220 – 1-7/8" squares

From assorted light prints, cut:

110 – 2-7/8" squares, cutting each in half diagonally for a total of 220 large triangles

220 – 1-1/2" x 2-1/2" rectangles

220 – 1-7/8" squares

110 – 1-1/2" squares

From dark brown print, cut:

90 – 4-1/2" setting squares

From orange print, cut:

10 – 7" squares, cutting each diagonally in an X for a total of 40 setting triangles

2 – 3-3/4" squares, cutting each in half diagonally for a total of 4 corner triangles

From brown print, cut:

7 – 5-1/2" x 42" border strips

From orange print, cut:

7 – 1-3/4" x 42" binding strips

From backing, cut:

2 – 40" x 73" rectangles

Assemble the Blocks

1. With right sides together, layer a dark print 1-7/8" square with a light print 1-7/8" square. Draw a diagonal line across the wrong side of the light print square.

2. Sew 1/4" on both sides of the drawn line. Cut apart on the drawn line. Press seam toward the dark triangle. The half-square triangles should measure 1-1/2" square. Repeat Steps 1 and 2 to make a total of 440 half-square triangles.

    MAKE 440
HALF-SQUARE TRIANGLES

3. Lay out four half-square triangles, one dark print large triangle, two dark print small triangles, two light print large triangles, two light print 1-1/2" x 2-1/2" rectangles, and one light print 1-1/2" square as shown. NOTE: There are a few blocks where the direction of the half-square triangles was changed to add interest.

4. Sew together one light print large triangle and one dark print large triangle. Press seam toward dark triangle. Sew half-square triangles together in pairs; add light print 1-1/2" square to one pair. Press seams in one direction. Sew these to the large triangles for the basket section.

5. Sew dark print small triangles to two light print 1-1/2" x 2-1/2" rectangles for left and right side sections. Press seams away from the small triangles. Sew side sections to basket section; press seams toward side sections. Add light print large triangle to complete one basket block. Press seam toward light triangle.

MAKE 110

6. Repeat Steps 3 - 5 to make a total of 110 basket blocks.

ASSEMBLE THE QUILT CENTER

1. Referring to Quilt Center Assembly Diagram, lay out 110 basket blocks, 90 dark brown 4-1/2" setting squares, and 38 orange print setting triangles in diagonal rows.
NOTE: There are two extra setting triangles.

2. Sew the pieces in each row together. Press seams toward the setting pieces.

3. Join rows. Press seams in one direction. Add orange print corner triangles to complete the quilt center. Press seams toward the corner triangles.

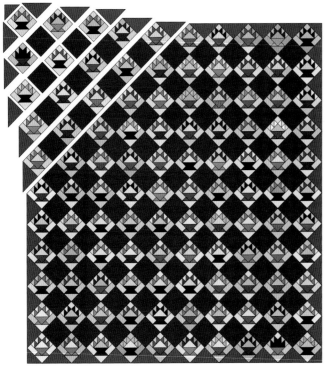

QUILT CENTER ASSEMBLY DIAGRAM

ADD THE BORDER

1. Piece the brown print 5-1/2" x 42" border strips to make the following: 2 – 5-1/2" x 70" for top and bottom and 2 – 5-1/2" x 75" for sides.

2. Center and sew a brown print 5-1/2" x 75" border strip to the left edge of the quilt center, beginning and ending the seam 1/4" from the corners of the quilt center as shown. Press seam toward the border. Attach the remaining 5-1/2" x 75" border strip to the opposite edge of the quilt center and the 5-1/2" x 70" border strips to the top and bottom edges in the same manner.

3. Place the quilt top right side up on your ironing board. Working with one corner at a time, extend the border ends out so the vertical strip overlaps the horizontal strip.

4. Lift up the vertical strip and fold it under itself at a 45-degree angle. Check the angle with a ruler and press.

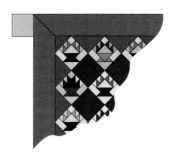

Lil' Baskets Quilt

5. With right sides together, fold the quilt on the diagonal so the edges of the two border strips line up. Pin and sew along the creased line from the inner point where the previous stitching ends to the outer edge of the border, backstitching to secure. Trim seam to 1/4". Press seam allowance open.

6. Repeat Steps 3 - 5 for remaining corners.

COMPLETE THE QUILT

1. Sew together the 40" x 73" backing rectangles along one long edge, using a 1/2" seam allowance. Press the seam allowance open.

2. Layer quilt top, batting, and pieced backing.

3. Quit as desired. Neutral thread was used to hand-quilt a 1" grid in the setting squares, triangles, and corners. The grid lines were continued in the border, curving from one setting triangle to the next. The blocks were stitched in-the-ditch.

4. Bind with orange print binding strips, referring to the Binding instructions on pages 12 - 13.

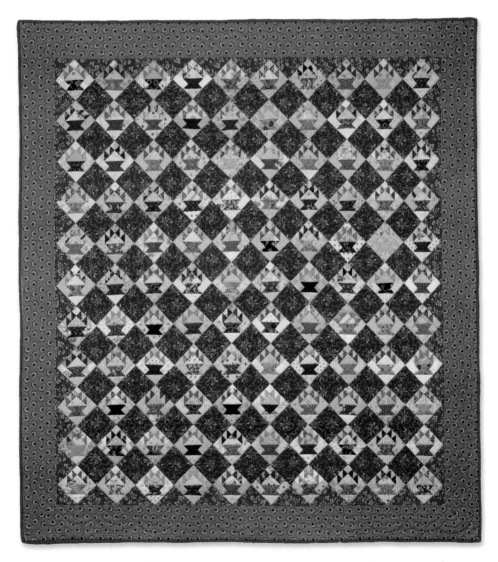

Designed and pieced by Edyta Sitar for Laundry Basket Quilts

Bubblegum, Bubblegum Quilt

Materials

- 1-1/4 yards total assorted dark prints for blocks
- 1 yard total assorted light-to-medium prints for blocks
- 1 yard pink print for setting squares and border
- 1/2 yard dark pink print for setting triangles and corner triangles
- 3/8 yard dark print for binding
- 3 yards backing fabric
- 51" square batting

Finished block: 5-3/4" square
Finished quilt: 45" square

Quantities are for 40/44"-wide, 100% cotton fabrics. Measurements include 1/4" seam allowances. Sew with right sides together unless otherwise stated.

Cut the Fabrics

NOTE: Most blocks were assembled using two fabrics. For a two-fabric block, cut:
2 – 3-1/8" squares, 2 – 2-3/8" squares, and 1 – 1-3/4" square from one dark print and 4 – 1-3/4" x 2-3/4" rectangles, 4 – 1-5/8" squares and 2 – 2-3/8" squares from one light-to-medium print. For a scrappier look, substitute other prints for some of the pieces.

From assorted dark prints, cut:
50 – 3-1/8" squares, cutting each in half diagonally for a total of 100 large triangles
50 – 2-3/8" squares, cutting each diagonally in an X for a total of 200 small triangles
25 – 1-3/4" center squares

From assorted light-to-medium prints, cut:
50 – 2-3/8" squares, cutting each diagonally in an X for a total of 200 small triangles
100 – 1-3/4" x 2-3/4" rectangles
100 – 1-5/8" corner squares

From pink print, cut:
16 – 6-1/4" setting squares
3 – 2-1/2" x 42" border strips
2 – 2-1/2" x 41" border strips

From dark pink print, cut:
4 – 9-3/8" squares, cutting each diagonally in an X for a total of 16 setting triangles
2 – 4-7/8" squares, cutting each in half diagonally for a total of 4 corner triangles

From dark print, cut:
5 – 1-3/4" x 42" binding strips

From backing, cut:
2 – 26" x 51" rectangles

Assemble the Blocks

1. Lay out one dark print 1-3/4" center square, four dark print large triangles, eight dark print small triangles, four light-to-medium print 1-3/4" x 2-3/4" rectangles, four light-to-medium print 1-5/8" corner squares, and eight light print small triangles as shown. Select these pieces from one dark print and one light-to-medium print, or vary the fabrics for a scrappier block.

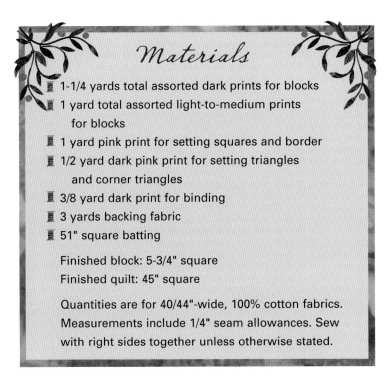

2. Sew the small triangles together in pairs of light and dark to make 4 of each pair. Press seams toward the dark triangles.

Make 4 of Each

3. Sew two pairs to adjacent sides of a light print 1-5/8" corner square as shown. Press seams toward square. Sew these to a dark print large triangle to complete one corner unit; press seam toward large triangle. Repeat to make four corner units.

Make 4

4. Sew the pieces together in rows. Press seams toward the light print rectangles. Sew the rows together. Press seams toward the rectangles.

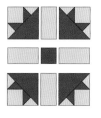

MAKE 25

5. Repeat Steps 1 - 4 to make a total of 25 blocks.

ASSEMBLE THE QUILT CENTER

1. Referring to the Quilt Center Assembly Diagram, lay out 25 blocks, 16 pink print 6-1/4" setting squares, and 16 dark pink print setting triangles in diagonal rows.

2. Sew the pieces in each row together. Press seams toward the setting pieces.

3. Join rows. Press seams in one direction. Add dark pink print corner triangles to complete the quilt center. Press seams toward the corner triangles. The quilt center should measure 41" square.

QUILT CENTER ASSEMBLY DIAGRAM

ADD THE BORDER

1. Referring to the Quilt Top Assembly Diagram, sew 2-1/2" x 41" border strips to opposite edges of the quilt center. Press seams toward border.

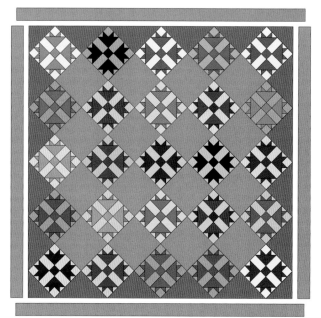

QUILT TOP ASSEMBLY DIAGRAM

2. Piece the 2-1/2" x 42" border strips to make two 2-1/2" x 45" border strips. Add these to the remaining edges. Press seams toward the border.

COMPLETE THE QUILT

1. Sew together the 26" x 51" backing rectangles along one long edge, using a 1/2" seam allowance. Press the seam allowance open.

2. Layer top, batting, and pieced backing.

3. Quilt as desired. Neutral thread was used to hand-quilt a 7/8" grid in the setting squares and 1/2" spaced diagonal lines in the border. The blocks are stitched in-the-ditch with an additional line of stitching in the dark large triangles. There is a grid-filled curved area in the inner corner of each setting and corner triangle with lines radiating outward.

4. Bind with dark print binding strips, referring to the Binding instructions on pages 12 - 13.

Bubblegum, Bubblegum Quilt
Designed and pieced by Edyta Sitar for Laundry Basket Quilts

FLEA MARKET TREASURE QUILT

Materials

- Variety of light 1-1/2" x 21" print and batik strips (approximately 90 strips)
- Variety of dark 1-1/2" x 21" print and batik strips (approximately 100 strips)
- 2-1/2 yards light gray batik for background, inner border, and middle border
- 1-1/4 yards dark gray batik for middle border and outer border
- 1/2 yard dark blue print for binding
- 1/2 yard total assorted gold-to-brown prints and batiks for stem appliqués
- Assorted green-to-brown print and batik scraps for leaf appliqués
- Assorted pink-to-burgundy print and batik scraps for tulip and bud appliqués
- Assorted gold print and batik scraps for blossom appliqués
- Assorted blue print and batik scraps for petal appliqués
- Red-and-black print scrap for flower center appliqués
- 4-1/2 yards backing fabric
- 79" square batting

Finished block: 48-1/4" square
Finished quilt: 73" square

Quantities are for 40/44"-wide, 100% cotton fabrics. Measurements include 1/4" seam allowances. Sew with right sides together unless otherwise noted.

CUT THE FABRICS

From light gray batik, cut:
1 – 21-1/4" square, cutting diagonally in an X for a total of 4 triangles
4 – 14-5/8" squares
9 – 7-1/4" squares, cutting each diagonally in an X for a total of 36 triangles
6 – 3-3/8" x 42" inner border strips

From dark gray batik, cut:
10 – 7-1/4" squares, cutting each diagonally in an X for a total of 40 triangles
4 – 4-3/4" squares
7 – 2-1/2" x 42" outer border strips

From dark blue print, cut:
8 – 1-3/4" x 42" binding strips
From backing, cut:
2 – 40" x 79" rectangles

ASSEMBLE THE QUILT CENTER

1. Sew together five light 1-1/2" x 21" print or batik strips and five dark 1-1/2" x 21" print or batik strips into a strip panel as shown. Offset each strip by 1" and alternate the light and dark strips. Repeat to make 10 strip panels.

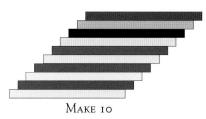

MAKE 10

2. Cut 1-1/2"-wide segments at a 45-degree angle across the strip panels as shown, cutting eight from each panel for a total of 80 segments.

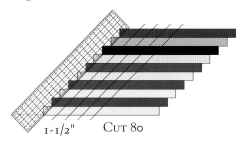

1-1/2"   CUT 80

3. Lay out 10 segments as shown. Sew the segments together to complete one diamond. Press seams in one direction. Repeat to make eight diamonds.

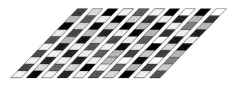

MAKE 8

111

4. Lay out the eight diamonds, four light gray batik 14-5/8" squares, and four light gray batik triangles as shown. Refer to 8-Pointed Star instructions on pages 6 - 11 to complete the single-block quilt center.

ADD THE BORDERS

1. Piece the light gray batik 3-3/8" x 42" inner border strips to make the following: 2 – 3-3/8" x 48-3/4" for top and bottom and 2 – 3-3/8" x 54-1/2" for sides.

2. Referring to the Quilt Top Assembly Diagram, sew the top and bottom inner border strips to the quilt center. Press seams toward border. Add the side inner border strips to the quilt center. Press seams toward border.

QUILT TOP ASSEMBLY DIAGRAM

3. Sew together two dark 1-1/2" x 21" print or batik strips and one light 1-1/2" x 21" print or batik strip into a strip panel as shown. Offset each strip by 1" and alternate the dark and light strips. Repeat to make 20 dark/light/dark strip panels.

MAKE 20

4. Cut 1-1/2"-wide segments at a 45-degree angle across the strip panel as shown, cutting eight from each panel for a total of 160 dark/light/dark segments.

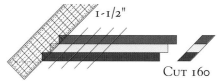

1-1/2"

CUT 160

5. Sew together two light 1-1/2" x 21" print or batik strips and one dark 1-1/2" x 21" print or batik strip into a strip panel as shown. Offset each strip by 1" and alternate the light and dark strips. Repeat to make 10 light/dark/light strip panels.

MAKE 10

6. Cut 1-1/2"-wide segments at a 45-degree angle across the strip panel as shown, cutting eight from each panel for a total of 80 light/dark/light segments.

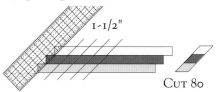

1-1/2"

CUT 80

7. Lay out two dark/light/dark segments and one light/dark/light segment as shown. Sew the segments together to complete one diamond. Press seams in one direction. Repeat to make 80 diamonds.

MAKE 80

8. For ease in piecing, mark the diamonds, 36 light gray batik triangles, 40 dark gray batik triangles, and four dark gray batik 4-3/4" squares. Use a ruler and pencil to lightly draw a line or dot to indicate the start and stopping points for the 1/4" set-in seams.

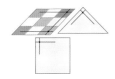

9. Sew two diamonds together in a pair as shown, stopping at the 1/4" seam allowance mark. Backstitch to secure seam ends. Press seam in one direction. Repeat to make 40 diamond pairs.

MAKE 40

10. Pin a dark gray batik triangle to one diamond in a diamond pair. Sew from the outside edge to the marked inner corner, backstitching to secure at the inner corner. Pin the adjacent diamond in the pair to the triangle. Sew from inner corner, backstitching to secure, to the outside edge. Press seams toward the triangle. Repeat to inset a dark gray batik triangle into each diamond pair for a total of 40 diamond/triangle units.

MAKE 40

11. Sew together the diamond/triangle units in four rows of 10 units as shown, sewing from the inner corner to the outside edge of the dark gray triangles.

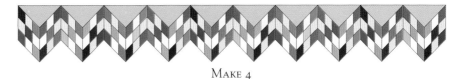

MAKE 4

12. Add nine light gray batik triangles to the remaining long edge of one row, using the same method as in Step 10. Repeat to make four pieced middle borders.

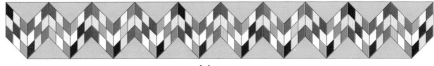

MAKE 4

13. Sew a pieced middle border to each edge of the quilt top, starting and stopping at the 1/4" seam allowance mark on the end diamonds.

14. Sew together the two diamonds that meet at each corner. Begin sewing at the tip of the diamond. Sew to the 1/4" mark, stop and backstitch.

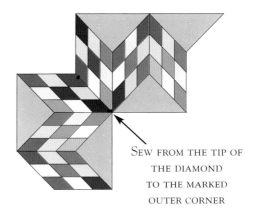

SEW FROM THE TIP OF
THE DIAMOND
TO THE MARKED
OUTER CORNER

15. Pin a dark gray batik 4-3/4" square to one diamond at the corner. Sew from the outside edge to the marked inner corner, backstitching to secure at the inner corner. Pin the adjacent diamond to the square. Sew from the inner corner, backstitching to secure, to the outside edge. Press seams toward the square. Repeat for each corner.

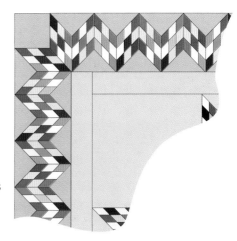

16. Piece the dark gray batik 2-1/2" x 42" outer border strips to make the following: 2 – 2-1/2" x 69" for top and bottom and 2 – 2-1/2" x 73" for sides.

17. Sew the top and bottom outer border strips to the quilt top. Press seams toward outer border. Add the side outer border strips to the quilt top. Press seams toward outer border.

Appliqué the Quilt

1. Trace the appliqué patterns on pages 115 - 116. Prepare the appliqué pieces using the instructions on pages 14 - 15 or the appliqué method of your choice.

From gold-to-brown prints and batiks, cut:
16 of pattern A (stem)

From green-to-brown prints and batiks, cut:
4 of pattern B (large leaf)
4 of pattern B reversed (large leaf)
8 of pattern C (leaf with stem)
8 of pattern D (double leaf)
24 of pattern E (medium leaf)
12 of pattern F (small leaf)
24 of pattern G (thin leaf)
16 of pattern H (small thin leaf)

From pink-to-burgundy print and batik scraps, cut:
12 *each* of pattern I (tulip)
12 of pattern J (tulip center)
4 of pattern K (bud base)
4 of pattern L (bud)

From gold print and batik scraps, cut:
4 of pattern M (flower center)
16 each of pattern N and O
    (blossom and small blossom)

From blue print and batik scraps, cut:
20 of pattern P (petal)

From red-and-black print scrap, cut:
4 of pattern Q (flower center)

2. Position the appliqué pieces on the quilt top, referring to the Quilt Top Diagram or the Appliqué Placement Diagram on page 117 as a guide. Appliqué the shapes in place using your favorite method. A narrow zigzag stitch was used along the edges of each of the appliqué pieces.

Complete the Quilt

1. Sew together the 40" x 79" backing rectangles along one long edge, using a 1/2" seam allowance. Press the seam allowance open.

2. Layer quilt top, batting, and pieced backing.

3. Quilt as desired. The quilt was stitched closely around the appliqué shapes. The 8-pointed star was stitched in-the-ditch at the outer edges and filled with a swirl pattern. The diamonds in the middle border were stitched in-the-ditch at the outer edges and filled with a feathered vine. An allover meandering design was used to fill all remaining areas of the quilt.

4. Bind with dark blue print binding strips, referring to the Binding instructions on pages 12 - 13.

QUILT TOP DIAGRAM

Flea Market Treasure Quilt Templates
These shapes have been reversed for fusible appliqué.

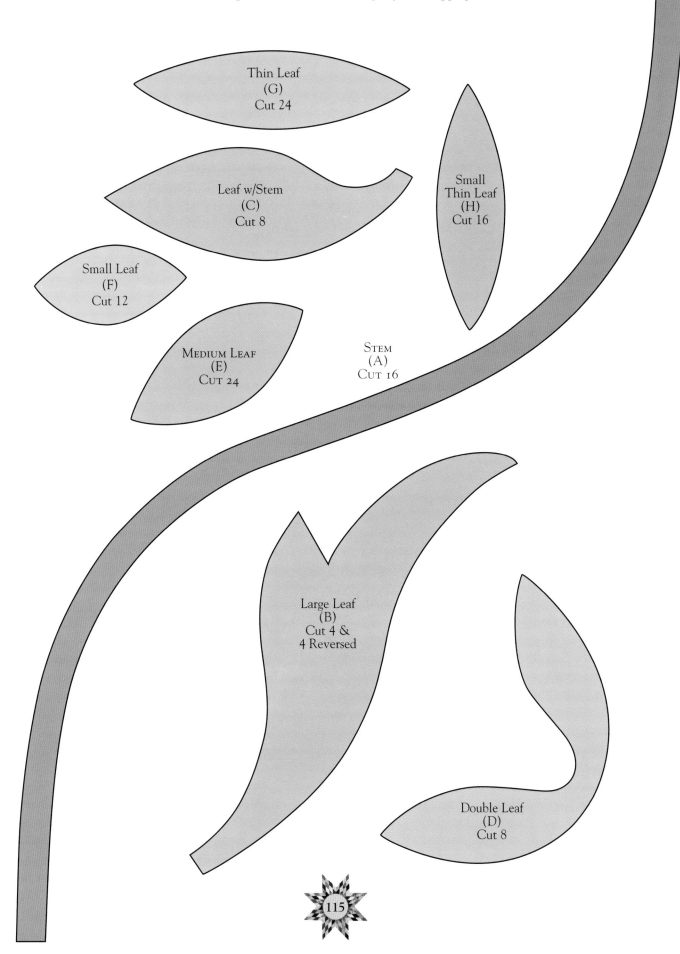

Thin Leaf
(G)
Cut 24

Leaf w/Stem
(C)
Cut 8

Small
Thin Leaf
(H)
Cut 16

Small Leaf
(F)
Cut 12

Medium Leaf
(E)
Cut 24

Stem
(A)
Cut 16

Large Leaf
(B)
Cut 4 &
4 Reversed

Double Leaf
(D)
Cut 8

FLEA MARKET TREASURE QUILT TEMPLATES
These shapes have been reversed for fusible appliqué.

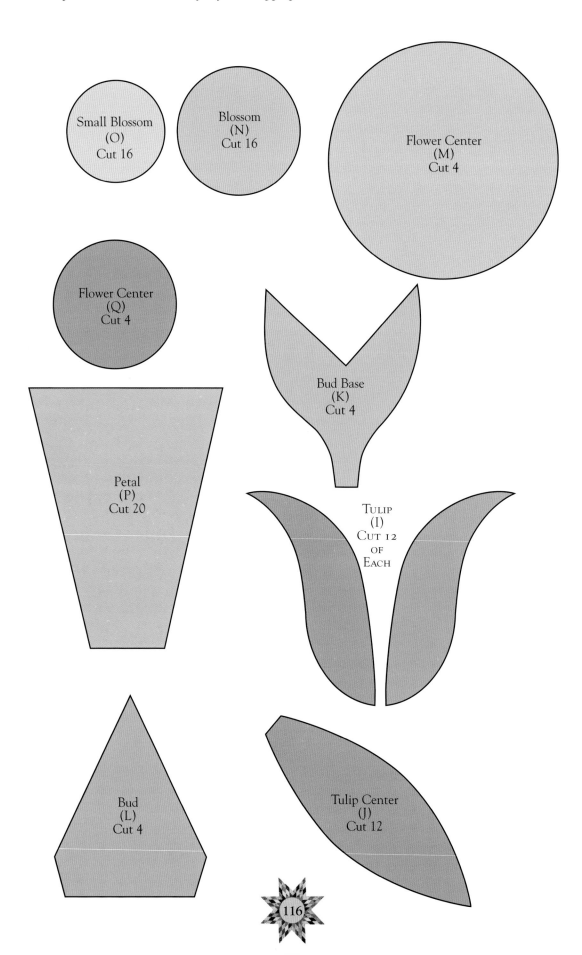

Small Blossom
(O)
Cut 16

Blossom
(N)
Cut 16

Flower Center
(M)
Cut 4

Flower Center
(Q)
Cut 4

Bud Base
(K)
Cut 4

Petal
(P)
Cut 20

TULIP
(I)
CUT 12
OF
EACH

Bud
(L)
Cut 4

Tulip Center
(J)
Cut 12

Flea Market Treasure Quilt
Designed and pieced by Edyta Sitar for Laundry Basket Quilts

Sometimes the journey ahead seems daunting, but small steps can add up to big accomplishments. Remember, the more difficult the path, the larger the reward.

Ice Cream Sandwiches Quilt

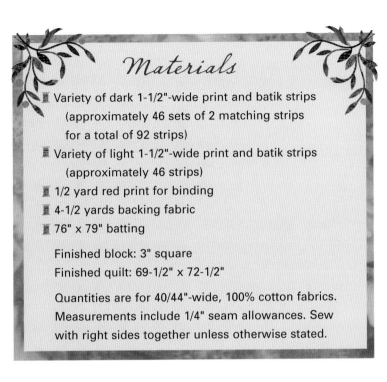

Materials

- Variety of dark 1-1/2"-wide print and batik strips (approximately 46 sets of 2 matching strips for a total of 92 strips)
- Variety of light 1-1/2"-wide print and batik strips (approximately 46 strips)
- 1/2 yard red print for binding
- 4-1/2 yards backing fabric
- 76" x 79" batting

Finished block: 3" square
Finished quilt: 69-1/2" x 72-1/2"

Quantities are for 40/44"-wide, 100% cotton fabrics. Measurements include 1/4" seam allowances. Sew with right sides together unless otherwise stated.

2. Cut a 3-1/2"-wide segment from the strip set to make one block. Continue cutting 3-1/2" wide segments from the strip set. Make enough dark/light/dark strip sets to cut 552 blocks.

3-1/2"

Assemble the Quilt Top

1. Referring to the Quilt Top Assembly Diagram, lay out 552 blocks in 24 horizontal rows alternating the position of the blocks as shown.
2. Sew the blocks in each row together. Press seams in one direction, alternating the direction from row to row.
3. Join rows. Press seams in one direction.

Cut the Fabric

From red print, cut:
7 – 1-3/4" x 42" binding strips
From backing cut:
2 – 38-1/2" x 79" rectangles

Make the Ice Cream Sandwich Blocks

1. Sew together two matching dark 1-1/2"-wide print or batik strips and one light 1-1/2"-wide print or batik strip to make a dark/light/dark strip set as shown. Press seams toward the dark strips.

Quilt Top Assembly Diagram

Ice Cream Sandwiches Quilt

COMPLETE THE QUILT

1. Sew together the 38-1/2" x 79" backing rectangles along one long edge, using a 1/2" seam allowance. Press the seam allowance open.
2. Layer quilt top, batting, and pieced backing.
3. Quilt as desired. The quilt was stitched using neutral thread for an allover flower pattern.
4. Bind with red print binding strips, referring to the Binding instructions on pages 12 - 13.

Designed and pieced by Edyta Sitar for Laundry Basket Quilts

No matter where you are from or where you are going, strangers become friends on the road of quilting. As you travel, visit your local quilt shop and make a new friend.

Square & Scrappy Quilt

Materials

- 2-1/2 yards total assorted light prints and batiks
- 2-1/2 yards total assorted dark prints and batiks
- 1/2 yard teal print for binding
- 3-1/2 yards backing fabric
- 63" square batting

Finished block: 8" square
Finished quilt: 56-1/2" square

Quantities are for 40/44"-wide, 100% cotton fabrics. Measurements include 1/4" seam allowances. Sew with right sides together unless otherwise stated.

CUT THE FABRICS

From assorted light prints and batiks, cut:
25 – 6-1/8" squares
98 – 2-7/8" squares
96 – 2-7/8" squares, cutting each in half
    diagonally for a total of 192 triangles

From assorted dark prints and batiks, cut:
24 – 6-1/8" squares
98 – 2-7/8" squares
100 – 2-7/8" squares, cutting each in
    half diagonally for a total of 200 triangles

From teal print, cut:
6 – 1-3/4" x 42" binding strips.

From backing, cut:
2 – 32" x 63" rectangles

ASSEMBLE THE BLOCKS

1. With right sides together, layer a light print 2-7/8" square with a dark print 2-7/8" square. Draw a diagonal line across the wrong side of the light print square.

2. Sew 1/4" on both sides of the drawn line. Cut apart on the drawn line. Press seams toward the dark triangle. The half-square triangles should measure 2-1/2" square. Repeat Steps 1 and 2 to make a total of 196 half-square triangles.

    MAKE 196

3. Join one triangle-square and two dark triangles to make a Dark Corner Unit as shown. Make 100 Dark Corner Units.

  MAKE 100

4. Join one triangle-square and two light triangles to make a Light Corner Unit. Make 96 Light Corner Units.

 MAKE 96

5. Lay out four Dark Corner Units and one light print or batik 6-1/8" square as shown. Join to complete one light block. Repeat to make 25 light blocks.

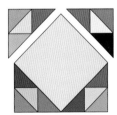 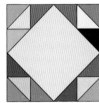
MAKE 25

6. Lay out four Light Corner Units and one dark print or batik 6-1/8" square as shown. Join to complete one dark block. Repeat to make 24 dark blocks.

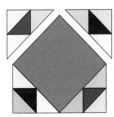 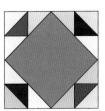
MAKE 24

Square & Scrappy Quilt

ASSEMBLE THE QUILT TOP

1. Refer to the Quilt Top Assembly Diagram to lay out 25 light blocks and 24 dark blocks in 7 horizontal rows, arranging the light and dark blocks in a checkerboard pattern.
2. Sew together blocks in each row. Press seams in one direction, alternating the direction from row to row.
3. Join rows. Press seams in one direction.

COMPLETE THE QUILT

1. Sew together the 32" x 63" backing rectangles along one long edge, using a 1/2" seam allowance. Press the seam allowance open.
2. Layer quilt top, batting, and pieced backing.
3. Quilt as desired. The quilt was stitched with neutral thread and an allover swirl pattern.
4. Bind with teal print binding strips, referring to the Binding instructions on pages 12 - 13.

QUILT TOP ASSEMBLY DIAGRAM

Square & Scrappy Quilt

Designed and pieced by Edyta Sitar for Laundry Basket Quilts

Acknowledgements

A very special "Thank You" is extended to the many skilled hands and patient minds that have helped me make this book possible:

▪ My loving family and friends who support me in everything I do, especially my mom, children, and husband, Mike.

▪ Moda Fabrics for the opportunity to design beautiful fabrics that are the starting point for my quilts. www.unitednotions.com

▪ Lolly's, Past Times Country Shop, and the community of Shipshewana, Indiana, where photography was taken.

▪ Creative Grids® for providing us with rulers that made the cutting easy and accurate. www.creativegridsusa.com

▪ Aurifil™ Threads for the most wonderful, beautiful threads that enhance my quilt designs. www.aurifil.com

▪ Hobbs Batting for adding beautiful drape to my quilts. www.hobbsbondedfibers.com

▪ The Landauer Publishing team for their patience, expertise and seemingly endless hours in bringing this book to life. Your hard work, sharing your talents, and always being accommodating will forever be one of my blessings. I thank you for that. www.landauercorp.com

▪ All the quilters who have enjoyed my designs over the years and exchanged strips and triangles with me, thank you so very much.

Edyta
www.laundrybasketquilts.com

Photography taken on location in Shipshewana, Indiana.

Photos on pages 32 and 91 taken at Past Times Country Shop.

Photo on page 119 taken at the Shipshewana Flea Market.

Photo on page 61 taken at The Davis Mercantile.

For more information on Shipshewana, Indiana or the Shipshewana Quilt Festival visit www.shipshewana.com.